Pronunciation Tasks

Pronunciation Tasks

A course for pre-intermediate students

Martin Hewings

TEACHER'S BOOK

CAMBRIDGE
UNIVERSITY PRESS

PUBLISHED BY THE PRESS SYNDICATE OF THE UNIVERSITY OF CAMBRIDGE
The Pitt Building, Trumpington Street, Cambridge, United Kingdom

CAMBRIDGE UNIVERSITY PRESS
The Edinburgh Building, Cambridge CB2 2RU, UK
40 West 20th Street, New York, NY 10011–4211, USA
477 Williamstown Road, Port Melbourne, VIC 3207, Australia
Ruiz de Alarcón 13, 28014 Madrid, Spain
Dock House, The Waterfront, Cape Town 8001, South Africa

http://www.cambridge.org

First published 1993
Sixth printing 2002

Printed in the United Kingdom at the University Press, Cambridge

ISBN 0 521 38610 1 Teacher's Book
ISBN 0 521 38611 X Student's Book
ISBN 0 521 38453 2 Set of 2 cassettes

Contents

Contents

Acknowledgements

I would like to thank:

Jeanne McCarten, Lindsay White and Alison Silver, who so professionally and patiently guided the book through its various stages.

Anne Colwell, Nick Newton and Nicholas Otway for their design work.

The many people who commented on the material and the principles on which it is based. In particular, Michael McCarthy, David Brazil and Richard Cauldwell.

Ann Hewings, Louise Ravelli, Thelma Smith and Peter Hickman who helped make recordings for earlier forms of the material.

The teachers and institutions who worked with the pilot edition, for their many helpful comments.

Key to phonetic symbols

Vowels

Symbol	Examples
/ɑː/	<u>ar</u>m p<u>ar</u>t
/æ/	<u>a</u>pple bl<u>a</u>ck
/aɪ/	<u>eye</u>s dr<u>i</u>ve
/aʊ/	<u>ou</u>t n<u>ow</u>
/e/	<u>e</u>nd p<u>e</u>n
/eɪ/	<u>eigh</u>t d<u>ay</u>
/eə/	<u>air</u> w<u>ear</u>
/ɪ/	<u>i</u>t s<u>i</u>t
/iː/	<u>ea</u>t s<u>ee</u>
/ɪə/	<u>ear</u> n<u>ear</u>
/ɒ/	<u>o</u>pposite st<u>o</u>p
/əʊ/	<u>o</u>pen ph<u>o</u>ne
/ɔː/	<u>a</u>lways m<u>ore</u>
/ɔɪ/	b<u>oy</u> j<u>oi</u>n
/ʊ/	w<u>ou</u>ld st<u>oo</u>d
/uː/	y<u>ou</u> ch<u>oose</u>
/ʊə/	s<u>ure</u> t<u>ou</u>rist
/ɜː/	<u>ear</u>ly b<u>ir</u>d
/ʌ/	<u>u</u>p l<u>u</u>ck
/ə/	<u>a</u>go doct<u>or</u>

Consonants

Symbol	Examples
/b/	<u>b</u>ed a<u>b</u>out
/d/	<u>d</u>o si<u>d</u>e
/f/	<u>f</u>ill sa<u>f</u>e
/g/	<u>g</u>ood bi<u>g</u>
/h/	<u>h</u>at be<u>h</u>ind
/j/	<u>y</u>es <u>y</u>ou
/k/	<u>c</u>at wee<u>k</u>
/l/	<u>l</u>ose a<u>ll</u>ow
/m/	<u>m</u>e la<u>m</u>p
/n/	<u>n</u>o a<u>n</u>y
/p/	<u>p</u>ut sto<u>p</u>
/r/	<u>r</u>un a<u>r</u>ound
/s/	<u>s</u>oon u<u>s</u>
/t/	<u>t</u>alk las<u>t</u>
/v/	<u>v</u>ery li<u>v</u>e
/w/	<u>w</u>in s<u>w</u>im
/z/	<u>z</u>oo love<u>s</u>
/ʃ/	<u>sh</u>ip pu<u>sh</u>
/ʒ/	mea<u>s</u>ure u<u>s</u>ual
/ŋ/	si<u>ng</u> hopi<u>ng</u>
/tʃ/	<u>ch</u>eap ca<u>tch</u>
/θ/	<u>th</u>in ba<u>th</u>
/ð/	<u>th</u>en o<u>th</u>er
/dʒ/	<u>J</u>une a<u>g</u>e

General introduction

1 Who is the book for?

Pronunciation Tasks is a set of supplementary materials designed to help elementary to intermediate level students improve their English pronunciation. Many of the activities will also be of use to more advanced level students.

It provides pronunciation work to supplement any general EFL or ESL course. Although it is primarily aimed at students working in class with a teacher, most of the activities could also be done by students working on their own with a cassette recorder.

2 Content

Traditional teaching focuses on the pronunciation of individual sounds. A poor English pronunciation is, however, often a result of many features of pronunciation – mispronounced sounds, inappropriate intonation, misplaced word stress, etc. *Pronunciation Tasks* gives attention to a number of important features. Each of the eight parts focuses on one of these features: vowels, consonants, consonant clusters, word stress and rhythm, changes that take place in conversational speech, intonation, the pronunciation of common grammatical items, and the relationships between spelling and pronunciation. Ways of checking and asking about pronunciation are also practised in Unit 1.

3 Order of use

Pronunciation Tasks provides very flexible material. Each of the eight parts is divided into eight or nine units. The units can be used in any order. Here are some of the ways you could use the material.

1 You could work through all 66 units from 1 to 66.

2 You could work through all 66 units, but in a different order. You might do this simply to add variety or to work first on the areas of pronunciation that seem to cause your students most problems.

You might do either 1 or 2 if you are teaching a class over a period of weeks and want to do some pronunciation work each day.

3 For shorter courses you might need to be selective in the sections of the material you use. You might decide, for example, that you only have time to use 30 of the units in your course. You could select these based on the likely problems of the students.

4 You could use selected parts or units of *Pronunciation Tasks* as problems arise with your students. For example, if you notice that students are having difficulties with word stress, you could work on some or all of the units in Part 4. If you notice that students are having problems producing a /v/ sound, you could work on Units 12 and 13.

4 Timing

Most units provide between about 15 and 25 minutes of teaching material, depending on such things as size of class and level of students. Some units contain activities where students are asked to give opinions, report answers to the rest of the class, and so on. Units like this may take longer than 30 minutes. You may find it useful to use half of a unit in one lesson and the rest in the next.

5 Methodology

A traditional approach to teaching pronunciation uses a three-step procedure: Discriminate + Repeat + Correct. So, for example, students are asked to discriminate between target sounds, then to repeat words or phrases that contain these sounds, and the teacher corrects where necessary. *Pronunciation Tasks* includes these activities, but tries also to vary the methodology. Students are asked to predict, identify, sort, match, work out rules, and exchange information. The activities are intended to help students to become more aware of their own English pronunciation and the pronunciation of native English speakers, to analyse pronunciation, and to produce certain features of pronunciation in relevant contexts.

The activities are 'task-based'. They normally require students to achieve something which **also** involves them in practising a particular feature of English pronunciation.

6 Using the recording

The symbol ▣ next to a task in the Student's Book means that the language for listening or repetition in the task is on the cassette. The symbol ◄◄ ▣ means that you should rewind the cassette and repeat the recording for the previous task. If the task requires students to repeat after the recording or to write something down after listening, pause the cassette to give students time to do this.

7 Monitoring

An important feature of the methodology recommended here involves **monitoring** students' pronunciation. Frequently in *Pronunciation Tasks* you are asked to **focus** on a particular feature of students' pronunciation and **correct** it if it is wrong. At these points, don't correct other pronunciation errors if they occur.

Some of the tasks are controlled, in that students are simply repeating given language. Here it is probably best to correct on the spot, stopping students and asking them, first, to try again and then, if they make the same mistake, to repeat after you. In less controlled tasks you may think that it is better to note the mistake and correct the student after the task is complete.

If appropriate for your students, encourage them to monitor each other's pronunciation. So, for example, in pairwork a student can monitor a particular feature of the partner's pronunciation, or you could appoint a third student to monitor the performing pair.

8 Vocabulary

Pronunciation Tasks tries to avoid using vocabulary that is unlikely to be known by students or that is not useful to them. The vocabulary that students have to use in the tasks tries to remain within a range that will probably be understood by pre-intermediate students, for example, the vocabulary introduced in *The New Cambridge English Course, Books 1* and 2 by Michael Swan and Catherine Walter.

9 Use of phonetic symbols

Phonetic symbols are frequently used to represent a sound. In most cases, however, example words are also given that include this sound, so no previous ability to read phonetic symbols is required either by you or the students. A reference key to the phonetic symbols used is provided in both the Student's and Teacher's Books.

10 Background and Extension notes

In the sections that follow, **Background** information about the pronunciation point is sometimes presented. Other notes give an **Extension** to the tasks in the unit. Some of these give ways of extending the task immediately above and others give a more general suggestion on how pronunciation practice might be provided.

11 Accents of English

The accent used most in the recordings is that of 'Southern British English' speakers. It is felt that as the material is likely to be used by students who have a wide range of first languages and motivations for learning English, this is the most appropriate accent on which students should model their own pronunciation.

However, to provide some exposure to a range of British English accents, recordings for some of the tasks are made by speakers with regional accents. Speakers with regional accents will only be found in *listening* tasks; where students are asked to repeat after the recording, they will repeat after a speaker of Southern British English.

12 Where to get more information

In the sections which follow, reference is made to a number of books that are useful in learning more about English pronunciation and about helping students overcome pronunciation difficulties.

RECOMMENDED BOOKS

Bradford, B. *Intonation in Context*, Cambridge University Press, 1988.
Brazil, D. *The Communicative Value of Intonation in English*, University of Birmingham, English Language Research, 1985.

Gimson, A.C. *An Introduction to the Pronunciation of English*, Edward Arnold, 1989, 4th edition.
Kenworthy, J. *Teaching English Pronunciation*, Longman, 1987.
Wells, J.C. *Longman Pronunciation Dictionary*, Longman, 1990.

In addition, a very useful source of information about the common pronunciation problems of students with particular first languages is:

Swan, M. & Smith, B. (eds) *Learner English: A teacher's guide to interference and other problems*, Cambridge University Press, 1987.

Introduction

In this unit, students are given some ways of asking how words are pronounced and checking that they can pronounce words correctly.

You could use it in one of two ways. You could refer students to it when they try to ask you about pronunciation but fail to do so in an appropriate way. Alternatively, you could teach the phrases before starting work on the material in the book.

Asking about the pronunciation of written words

1 Ask students to listen to the conversations and to focus on the phrases in **bold**.

2 Students work in pairs and ask each other about the pronunciation of the words given. The five words all appear in later units.

An alternative way to practise these phrases is to write a number of words on the blackboard that students are unlikely to know. Students come to the board, point to a word, and ask you about its pronunciation.

Another possibility is to write some difficult words on pieces of paper and distribute one to each student. Students ask each other how to pronounce the words, and reply using the phrases given.

Asking if your pronunciation is correct

3 Ask students to listen to the conversations and to focus on the phrases in **bold**.

4 Students work in pairs and ask each other about the pronunciation of the place names given.

An alternative way to practise these phrases is to write some place names from Britain or the USA on the blackboard. Choose individual students to have a short conversation with you as in the Student's Book.

Asking which pronunciation is correct

5 Ask students to listen to the conversations and to focus on the phrases in **bold**. Point out that for the words 'either' and 'often' there are two possible pronunciations and that it doesn't matter which they choose. You could ask students to make similar conversations using other words for which there are alternative pronunciations, such as:

again /əgen/ or /əgeɪn/
schedule /ʃedjuːl/ or /skedjuːl/
Monday /mʌndeɪ/ or /mʌndɪ/ (and other days of the week)

ate /eɪt/ or /et/
nephew /nefjuː/ or /nevjuː/

6 To practise, students ask you similar questions about the pronunciation of words they are unsure of. Alternatively, write words on the blackboard that you know cause problems for the students and have them ask you about their pronunciation using the phrase in **5**.

Part 1 Vowels

Aims and organisation

In Part 1 students practise the pronunciation of **vowels**. Attention is focused on differences in the **lengths** of vowels (short vowels versus long vowels) and the distinction between **simple vowels** (or monophthongs) and **diphthongs**.

Unit 2
/æ/ (as in <u>a</u>pple), /ɪ/ (<u>i</u>t) and /e/ (<u>e</u>nd)   (Short vowels)

Unit 3
/ɒ/ (st<u>o</u>p), /ʊ/ (w<u>ou</u>ld) and /ʌ/ (<u>u</u>p)   (Short vowels)

Unit 4
(i) /ɪ/ and /e/, and (ii) /æ/ and /ʌ/   (Short vowels contrasted)

Unit 5
/iː/ (<u>ea</u>t), /ɜː/ (<u>ear</u>ly), /ɑː/ (<u>ar</u>m), /ɔː/ (m<u>ore</u>) and /uː/ (y<u>ou</u>)   (Long vowels)

Unit 6
(i) /æ/ and /ɑː/, and (ii) /ɪ/ and /iː/   (Short and long vowels contrasted)

Unit 7
(i) /ʌ/, /ʊ/ and /uː/, and (ii) /ɒ/ and /ɔː/   (Short and long vowels contrasted)

Unit 8
/eɪ/ (<u>eigh</u>t), /aɪ/ (dr<u>i</u>ve), /əʊ/ (<u>o</u>pen) and /aʊ/ (<u>ou</u>t)   (Diphthongs)

Unit 9
(i) /eɪ/ and /e/, and (ii) /əʊ/ and /ɔː/   (Diphthongs and simple vowels contrasted)

General notes

The units in Part 1 are of two types. Units 2, 3, 5 and 8 present and give practice in vowels which share a particular feature. The remaining units deal with particular sound contrasts that are frequently problematic. By organising the material in this way, it is hoped to give both general practice in producing the main categories of vowels, and also to provide the opportunity for more detailed practice of troublesome vowel contrasts.

Notice that not all the vowel sounds of English are practised here. The other diphthongs (/ʊə/, /eə/, /ɪə/ and /ɔɪ/) and the 'diphthong + /ə/ ' sounds (/aɪə/ (as in _fire_) and /aʊə/ (as in _our_) are not dealt with because they occur infrequently in the most common words of English. They may, however, be a problem for your students. If they are, you could adapt some of the activities in Part 1 to provide practice of these sounds. Some suggestions on which activities you could adapt are given in the notes below.

/ə/ is not specifically practised here, because it is dealt with at various other points in later parts of the book, particularly Part 4, Unit 31 and Part 8, Unit 63.

> **Background**
>
> Vowels are traditionally classified in one of two ways: into simple vowels and diphthongs (glides between vowels); or into short vowels and long vowels (which include diphthongs and those vowels, like /uː/, which have a : symbol after them in the phonetic alphabet). These classifications are used in organising the material in Part 1. The short / long vowel distinction is a simplification, however, and not all 'long' vowels are longer than short vowels. There is more information on this and a suggestion on how to make students aware of this fact in the notes for Unit 6.

Notes on each unit

Unit 2 The short vowels /æ/, /ɪ/ and /e/

1 Monitor the pronunciation of the vowel /æ/ in these words.

2 & 3 *Answers*
A: Where were you st<u>a</u>nding?
B: Outside my fl<u>a</u>t.
A: Where was the m<u>a</u>n?
B: He r<u>a</u>n out of the b<u>a</u>nk.
A: Was he c<u>a</u>rrying anything?
B: A bl<u>a</u>ck b<u>a</u>g.
A: Th<u>a</u>nk you, m<u>a</u>dam.

4 Rewind and repeat. Pause at the end of each line to give students time to repeat. During repetition and pairwork, monitor the /æ/ sounds underlined.

5a *Answers*
A: Th<u>i</u>s one?
B: A b<u>i</u>t b<u>i</u>g.
A: Let's g<u>i</u>ve her th<u>i</u>s one, then.
B: St<u>i</u>ll too b<u>i</u>g.

A: Will this fit?

B: Yes, I think so. She's quite thin.

Rewind and repeat as above. Monitor the /ɪ/ sounds underlined.

Notice that the usual pronunciation of 'she' in a context is /ʃɪ/. If the word is said on its own, or if it is meant to show a contrast (for example, in 'I didn't do it, *she* did!') then it is pronounced /ʃiː/.

b *Answers*

A: And can you get some eggs?

B: How many?

A: Ten, please.

B: Anything else?

A: Some bread. Do you need any money?

B: No I'll pay by cheque.

Rewind and repeat as above. Monitor the /e/ sounds underlined.

> **Extension**
>
> Ask students to find examples where the letters 'a', 'i' and 'e' *don't* represent the sounds /æ/, /ɪ/ and /e/ respectively.
>
> (In **2** 'a' is pronounced /ə/ in *was*, *a*, and *madam*; and pronounced /e/ in *anything*. In **5a** 'i' is pronounced /aɪ/ in *I* and *quite*. In **5b** 'e' is not pronounced in *some, please, else* and *cheque*; and pronounced /iː/ with the letter 'a' in *please*, with the letter 'y' in *money*, and with 'ee' in *need*.)
>
> Ask students to note how many ways each of the three sounds can be spelt.
>
> (In **2** /æ/ is spelt only 'a'. In **5a** /ɪ/ is usually spelt 'i', but is spelt 'e' in *she's*. In **5b** /e/ is spelt 'e', 'a' (*many, anything* and *any*) and 'ea' (*bread*).)

6 The items in the box all include at least one of the target vowels /æ/, /ɪ/ or /e/. These are underlined here.

a camera   a television   a handbag   a credit card
a stamp   a swimming costume   a tennis racket   a hat
a sweater   a fishing rod   some cash   a chess set
some matches   a map   a tent   your address book
a blanket   some string

6, 7 & 8 Monitor the target vowels during repetition, discussion and reporting back.

> **Extension**
>
> Ask students to collect the names of one thing that it would be useful to have when: (a) cooking a meal, (b) building a house, and (c) climbing a mountain. Each word must contain the sound /æ/, /ɪ/ or /e/. Ask them to report back and monitor the pronunciation of these vowels. Make a note of the words and use them in a later lesson in a task similar to that in **6** to **8**.

Unit 3 The short vowels /ɒ/, /ʊ/ and /ʌ/

1 *Answers*

w<u>a</u>tch/st<u>o</u>pped	just/l<u>u</u>nch	bl<u>oo</u>d/c<u>u</u>t
l<u>oo</u>ks/g<u>oo</u>d	g<u>o</u>t/c<u>ou</u>gh	n<u>o</u>t/l<u>o</u>ng
sh<u>u</u>t/st<u>u</u>ck	p<u>u</u>ll/p<u>u</u>sh	c<u>oo</u>k/b<u>oo</u>k

2 Monitor the pronunciation of the vowels in these words.

3 *Answers*

1 A: What time is it?
   B: Sorry, my <u>watch</u> has <u>stopped</u>.
2 A: Aren't you well?
   B: No, I've <u>got</u> a <u>cough</u>.
3 A: What time's the bus?
   B: <u>Not</u> <u>long</u> now.
4 A: Do you like it?
   B: Yes, it <u>looks</u> <u>good</u>.
5 A: Can't you <u>shut</u> the door?
   B: No, it's <u>stuck</u>.
6 A: Is that <u>blood</u>?
   B: Yes, I <u>cut</u> my finger.
7 A: Is Tom here?
   B: No, he's <u>just</u> gone for <u>lunch</u>.
8 A: What are you reading?
   B: It's a <u>cook</u> <u>book</u>.
9 A: I can't open the door.
   B: <u>Pull/Push</u> it, don't <u>push/pull</u> it!

5 Monitor the pronunciation of the vowels in the words underlined in **3**.

6 & 7 The adjectives all contain target vowels /ɒ/, /ʊ/ and /ʌ/. Some suggestions are: g<u>oo</u>d (book, holiday, film); c<u>o</u>mfortable (bed, seat, shoes); h<u>o</u>rrible (dream, journey, picture); f<u>u</u>nny (TV programme, joke, story).

   Monitor the underlined vowels in discussion and reporting back.

> **Extension**
>
> If students have problems with other vowel (or consonant) sounds, you could provide practice by adapting this task. For example, if you want to practise the diphthongs /aɪ/ (as in dr<u>i</u>ve) and /eɪ/ (as in d<u>ay</u>), use adjectives containing these sounds, such as n<u>i</u>ce, exc<u>i</u>ting, k<u>i</u>nd, and d<u>a</u>ngerous, f<u>a</u>mous, str<u>a</u>nge.

Unit 4 /ɪ/ & /e/ and /æ/ & /ʌ/

Focus on /ɪ/ and /e/

1 Monitor the pronunciation of the vowels in the words.

2 Monitor pronunciation as in **1**. If students have difficulty in hearing or producing a difference between /ɪ/ and /e/ in the words, offer help. Demonstrate a word with either /ɪ/ or /e/ and ask the student to decide which vowel it contains. When they get it right, ask them to repeat after you. For further suggestions you might look at Kenworthy's *Teaching English Pronunciation*.

> **Extension**
>
> You could adapt the task in **1** and **2** to provide practice in producing and discriminating between any pairs of sounds, either pairs of vowels or pairs of consonants.

3 Sentences on the recording are as follows. Words from the boxes are underlined and the answers given at the end.

1 Go to the <u>lift</u>, and then go up to the sixth floor. (A)
2 They <u>fell</u> in a hole in the road. (B)
3 You'll be late as <u>well</u>, Tom. (B)
4 You don't <u>spell</u> 'orange juice' like that. (B)
5 Wait <u>till</u> I come home. (A)
6 Can you <u>let</u> me have a cigarette? (B)
7 It was too expensive to buy <u>ten</u>. (B)
8 Can I have the <u>bill</u>, please? (A)

Focus on /æ/ and /ʌ/

4 *Answers* (target vowels are underlined)

/æ/ + /ʌ/	/ʌ/ + /æ/	/ʌ/ + /ʌ/	/æ/ + /æ/
St<u>a</u>nd <u>u</u>p!	A h<u>u</u>ngry c<u>a</u>t.	S<u>o</u>mewhere s<u>u</u>nny.	A bl<u>a</u>ck j<u>a</u>cket.
A j<u>a</u>zz cl<u>u</u>b.	A c<u>o</u>mpany m<u>a</u>nager.	H<u>u</u>rry <u>u</u>p!	A tr<u>a</u>ffic j<u>a</u>m.
	A g<u>u</u>n f<u>a</u>ctory.	A l<u>u</u>cky n<u>u</u>mber.	A pl<u>a</u>stic b<u>a</u>g.
		N<u>o</u>thing m<u>u</u>ch.	

5 On the recording the answers are given in the order in the table above. That is, first the phrases in column one, then the phrases in column two, and so on. This allows students to check their answers as they repeat. Monitor the pronunciation of the vowels underlined in **4**.

6 *Most likely answers*

1 What did you do at the weekend? Nothing much.
2 What's her job? A company manager.
3 What was he wearing? A black jacket.
4 Where did you go last night? A jazz club.
5 Where do you work? A gun factory.
6 Hurry up! I'm coming as fast as I can!
7 What made you late? A traffic jam.

7 Monitor the pronunciation of the vowels underlined in **4**.

Unit 5 The long vowels /iː/, /ɜː/, /ɑː/, /ɔː/ and /uː/

1 *Answers*

1	clean	/iː/	visa, piece, me, free
2	bird	/ɜː/	prefer, early, Thursday, word
3	car	/ɑː/	heart, laugh, banana, half
4	four	/ɔː/	law, water, abroad, bought
5	food	/uː/	improve, fruit, June, blue

> **Extension**
>
> Draw students' attention to the fact that each of these long vowel sounds can be spelt in different ways. Ask students to find one *more* word that contains each spelling. For example, for /iː/ they might have police, believe, be, see.

2 Monitor the pronunciation of the long vowels in the words.

3 & 4 *Answers*

1 A: Have you <u>seen</u> my niece?
  B: Is she the girl in the <u>skirt</u>?
2 A: Do you like my <u>blue</u> boots?
  B: I prefer the <u>purple</u> ones.
3 A: When did you lose your <u>suitcase</u>?
  B: Last <u>March</u>.
4 A: What did he do when he saw the <u>report</u>?
  B: He started to <u>laugh</u>.
5 A: It's his birthday on the <u>third</u>, isn't it?
  B: Yes. I've bought him a <u>portable</u> TV.
6 A: Where did your <u>father</u> leave the car?
  B: It's parked in the <u>car</u> <u>park</u>.

4 & 5 During repetition monitor the long vowel sounds.

> **Extension**
>
> For better students, write some imaginary newspaper headlines that include words with the long vowels practised in Unit 5. For example:
>
> "CHEAPER IMPORTS BY JUNE," SAYS PM
>
> EMERGENCY WORKERS RESCUE THIRTY
>
> NEW COMPUTER TO BEAT THIEVES
>
> MP IN SUPERMARKET ARGUMENT
>
> Ask students to work in pairs and to make up a brief story that might come after each headline. Then they tell their stories to the rest of the class. In discussion and reporting back, monitor target long vowels.

Unit 6 /æ/ & /ɑː/ and /ɪ/ & /iː/

Focus *on /æ/ and /ɑː/*

> **Background**
>
> In England, the vowel sound /ɑː/ is often used by speakers from the south
> east when speakers from the north use /æ/. (The situation in the south
> west of England is more variable.) This distinction happens particularly in
> words where the letter 'a' comes before the sounds /f/, /θ/ and /s/
> (voiceless fricatives) and before certain consonant clusters beginning with
> the sounds /m/ or /n/. Many speakers in Britain may not have a strong
> regional accent, but their use of /ɑː/ or /æ/ in these contexts marks them as
> coming from the south east or not.

1 *Answers*

1	b<u>a</u>throom /æ/	(B)	7	p<u>a</u>ssport /ɑː/	(A)
2	gl<u>a</u>sses /æ/	(B)	8	f<u>a</u>st /æ/	(B)
3	d<u>a</u>nce /ɑː/	(A)	9	<u>a</u>fter /æ/	(B)
4	<u>a</u>sk /ɑː/	(A)	10	p<u>a</u>st /æ/	(B)
5	l<u>a</u>st /æ/	(B)	11	p<u>a</u>th /ɑː/	(A)
6	<u>a</u>nswer /ɑː/	(A)	12	<u>a</u>fternoon /ɑː/	(A)

Focus *on /ɪ/ and /iː/*

2 Monitor the pronunciation of /ɪ/ (as in <u>I</u>ndia) and /iː/ (as in sw<u>ee</u>ts).

3 *Possible answers*

1	Things to eat	sweets and chicken
2	Numbers	fourteen and a million
3	Things containing water	river and stream
4	Jobs	builder and teacher
5	Parts of the body	knee and finger
6	Places where people live	street and city
7	Holiday times	Christmas and Easter
8	Countries	India and Egypt
9	Nationalities	Swedish and British
10	Things to drink	milk and tea

4 Monitor the pronunciation of /ɪ/ and /iː/.

> **Background**
>
> The length of the long vowels and diphthongs tends to vary depending
> on the sound which comes after them. In stressed syllables, if a long vowel
> comes before an unvoiced consonant (/p/, /t/, /k/, /tʃ/, /f/, /θ/, /s/ or /ʃ/) it
> tends to be shorter than if it is followed by a voiced consonant or no
> consonant. Compare, for example, l<u>i</u>tre/l<u>ea</u>der, r<u>oo</u>t/r<u>u</u>de, s<u>aw</u>/s<u>or</u>t.
>
> If appropriate for your students, you could devise a task to make them
> aware of this. Give them a list of words all containing the sound /iː/ in the
> stressed syllable. Make sure that some are followed by voiced consonants

and some by unvoiced. You could select words from Unit 6 and perhaps add a few more of your own, or ask students to provide you with a few. Ask them to decide which /iː/ sounds are relatively long and which are relatively short, and why. Give a hint about the following consonant if necessary. Students might either sound out the words themselves, or you could read out the list, or record it on tape and allow students access to the recording as data to be investigated.

Unit 7 /ʌ/, /ʊ/ & /uː/ and /ɒ/ & /ɔː/

Focus on /ʌ/, /ʊ/ and /uː/

1

/ʌ/	/ʊ/	/uː/
e.g. sun	e.g. would	e.g. two
customer	full	include
gun	pull	supermarket
Sunday	put	June
number	push	flu

2 On the recording the words including /ʌ/ are said first, then the words with /ʊ/ and then the words with /uː/. During repetition monitor /ʌ/, /ʊ/ and /uː/.

3 *Answers*
   a) 6 & 2   b) 1 & 7   c) 8 & 3   d) 9 & 4   e) 10 & 5

4 During repetition and pairwork monitor the pronunciation of /ʌ/, /ʊ/ and /uː/.

5   /ʊ/   /ʌ/
   1 Where shall I put your luggage?

                                /uː/ /uː/   /uː/
   2 But I bought a new tube on Tuesday.

            /uː/   /ʌ/   /ʌ/
   3 It's too hot. It's a lovely sunny day.

         /ʌ/   /ʊ/   /uː/   /uː/   /uː/ /uː/
   4 My uncle. Would you like me to introduce you?

                           /ʊ/   /ʊ/   /ʊ/
   5 It's from a really good cook book.

                        /ʌ/   /ʊ/
   6 There isn't much toothpaste left.

            /uː/   /ʌ/   /uː/
   7 In the boot. There's just a suitcase.

/ʊ/   /ʊ/ /ʌ/
8 I think I'll p<u>u</u>t on my w<u>oo</u>llen j<u>u</u>mper.

/uː/   /uː/ /uː/
9 Wh<u>o</u>'s that in the bl<u>ue</u> s<u>ui</u>t?

/ʌ/   /uː/   /ʌ/
10 That <u>o</u>nion s<u>ou</u>p was w<u>o</u>nderful.

Notice that 'to' in sentence 4 could also be pronounced /tə/.

Extension

Tell students that there are four spellings that can be pronounced /ʌ/ in some words, /ʊ/ in others and /uː/ in others. Draw this table on the board and ask them to write one word in each space. The word should include the spelling given on the left and the sound given along the top.

		Sound		
		/ʌ/	/ʊ/	/uː/
	oo			
Spelling	o			
	ou			
	u			

For example, the top row could be:
blood   look   room
Encourage students to find words that are *not* used in Unit 7. Collect the words and use them later in a task similar to that in **1**.

Focus on /ɒ/ and /ɔː/

6 Monitor the pronunciation of the underlined vowels.

7 Check that your students can produce the correct question forms. To do this, have them ask you the questions first and, if necessary, write the questions on the board.

Extension

You could adapt this task to provide practice of other vowels or consonants that are a problem for your students.

Unit 8 The long vowels /eɪ/, /aɪ/, /əʊ/ and /aʊ/

Extension

You could briefly explain to students that vowels are sometimes divided into simple vowels and diphthongs. The sounds that are practised in this unit are diphthongs. Say that diphthongs are 'combinations' of two vowels or vowel sounds that move from one simple vowel sound to another and are generally longer than vowels such as /ɪ/, /e/, /æ/, and so on. The symbols for diphthongs contain two simple vowel symbols.

1 Monitor the pronunciation of the vowels underlined.

2 *Answers*

	/eɪ/	/aɪ/	/əʊ/	/aʊ/
1	1	0	3	1
2	4	1	0	0
3	1	0	1	3
4	0	4	0	1
5	2	0	2	1
6	0	3	1	1

3 When students give corrections, monitor the diphthongs /eɪ/, /aɪ/, /əʊ/ and /aʊ/ in the 'corrected' words (July, phone, Joan, house, etc.).

Text (with correct version in brackets)
One morning last April (July), Joan was lying in bed when the doorbell (phone) rang. It was her friend, Dave, who invited her out for a picnic at the seaside. Later that day Jean (Joan) left her flat (house) and drove (rode) her car (bike) to the bus (railway) station to catch the bus (train). She was wearing a T-shirt and skirt (coat and trousers) as it was quite hot (cold). As she sat on the bus (train) she looked out of the door (window). The sun was shining (It was cloudy). She saw a plane going over a forest (mountain) and some horses (cows) in the fields. Before long she arrived at the river (seaside) and met Steve (Dave). They went down to the beach and had their picnic next to a rock (boat). They had sandwiches and crisps (cake and ice cream), and Steve (Dave) painted a picture (took some photos). They had a lovely day.

4 & 5 During pairwork monitor the pronunciation of the diphthongs in the corrected words.

Extension
You could practise almost any problem vowel or consonant sound in a similar way. Make up a short story which includes words containing the problem sound. Tell the story to the class and ask them to try to remember as much of it as they can. Then retell it, but substitute other words for those containing the problem sounds. Students stop you when they hear something different from the first version and give a correction using the same pattern as in **4**. Check that they are pronouncing the problem vowel correctly.

Unit 9 /eɪ/ & /e/ and /əʊ/ & /ɔː/

Focus on /eɪ/ and /e/

1 & 2 *Answers*

potato	dentist	Belgium	November	seven	eight
sailor	radio	train	Asia	May	sweater	Spain
yellow	table	grey	head	helicopter	South America
bed	embassy	bread	television	dress	brain
station						

2 Monitor the pronunciation of the vowels /eɪ/ and /e/.

3 *Possible answers*
potato + bread (things to eat)
dentist + sailor (jobs)
Belgium + Spain (countries)
November + May (months)
seven + eight (numbers)
radio + television (media/use electricity)
train + helicopter (means of transport)
Asia + South America (continents)
sweater + dress (items of clothing)
yellow + grey (colours)
table + bed (items of furniture)
head + brain (parts of the body)
embassy + station (buildings)

4 Monitor the pronunciation of the vowels /eɪ/ and /e/.

> **Extension**
> Better students could also be asked to explain *what* the pairs of words have in common.

Focus on /əʊ/ and /ɔː/

5 Monitor the pronunciation of the underlined vowels.

6 & 7 Students can either work in pairs first before reporting their answers, or can work and report individually. Try to elicit, by questioning, some of the target sounds in the marked words below if the students don't include them in their descriptions. For example: 'Where's the wardrobe?' (In the corner) or 'What's in the corner?' (A wardrobe). Monitor the target sounds /əʊ/ and /ɔː/.
  Words including /əʊ/ or /ɔː/ that could be used to describe the pictures are given overleaf.

Picture 1
A wardrobe in the corner with an open door; clothes inside the wardrobe; a coat on the back of the wardrobe door; man walking through bedroom door; girl at table, drawing; table with a drawer; ball on floor; window; snow through window.

Picture 2
Crossroads; men digging hole in road; coach; motorbike; post office, hotel, shop with 'Closed' sign; phone box; chimney with smoke coming out; it's autumn; it's a quarter past four; old man walking along – bald, wrapped up warmly against the cold.

Part 2 Consonants

Aims and organisation

In Part 2 students practise the pronunciation of **consonants**.

Unit 10
/p/, /b/, /t/, /d/, /k/ and /g/

Unit 11
(i) /t/ and /d/, and (ii) /p/ and /b/

Unit 12
/s/, /z/, /f/, /v/, /θ/ (as in <u>th</u>in) and /ð/ (<u>th</u>en)

Unit 13
(i) /θ/ and /ð/, and (ii) /v/, /f/ and /b/

Unit 14
/ʃ/ (<u>sh</u>ip), /tʃ/ (<u>ch</u>eap), /ʒ/ (mea<u>s</u>ure) and /dʒ/ (<u>J</u>une)

Unit 15
(i) /ʃ/ and /tʃ/, and (ii) /dr/ and /tr/

Unit 16
/w/, /r/, /j/ (<u>y</u>es) and /l/

Unit 17
(i) /w/ and /v/, and (ii) /r/ and /l/

Unit 18
/m/, /n/ and /ŋ/ (si<u>ng</u>)

The units in Part 2 are of two types. Units 10, 12, 14, 16 and 18
present and give practice in groups of consonants which share a certain
feature of pronunciation. Units 11, 13, 15 and 17 contrast sounds that
many learners either have difficulties hearing a difference between, or
producing a difference between. By organising the material in this way,
it is hoped to give both general practice in producing the main
categories of consonants, and also to provide the opportunity for more
detailed practice of troublesome consonant contrasts. You may find
that only some of the sound contrasts in Units 11, 13, 15 and 17 are
difficult for your students. Be selective and work only on those that
pose a problem.
  More information on the similarities and differences between the

sounds looked at is given below at the beginning of the notes on each unit.

General notes

Each of Units 10, 12, 14, 16 and 18 begins with lists of words for repetition which include the target sounds for that unit. Where possible they are presented in word-initial position and followed by a vowel to avoid any problems that consonant clusters might present. This initial presentation allows the target sounds to be identified for the learners, allows the phonetic symbols to be clearly introduced, and provides short 'checklists' which you could guide students back to if they have special problems in producing a particular sound.

In the practice material which follows these presentations, the sounds in focus are not, however, always presented in initial position. While it is recognised that the production of the sounds may vary in detail when the immediate context changes, at this level it is felt that it would be an unnecessary complication to draw attention to this.

Notes on each unit

Unit 10 /p/, /b/, /t/, /d/, /k/ and /g/

> **Background**
>
> The consonants practised in this unit are sometimes referred to as 'stop' consonants or 'plosive' consonants. In all of them there is a build up of air behind a 'closure' at some point in the mouth, and then a sudden release of the air.

1 Monitor the pronunciation of the underlined consonants.

2 *Answers*
   a) /k/ and /g/   b) /t/ and /d/   c) /p/ and /b/

   You could go on to ask students how it is that for each picture *two* sounds are shown. Try to elicit that one sound is *voiced* and the other *unvoiced* in each pair.

> **Background**
>
> Voiced sounds are those produced with the vocal folds vibrating rapidly as the air passes between them from the lungs. All vowels, and consonants such as /b/, /d/ and /g/ are produced in this way. Unvoiced or 'voiceless' sounds such as /p/, /t/ and /k/ are produced with the vocal folds open and with little or no vibration.
>
>   To demonstrate the difference between voiced and unvoiced sounds, tell students to place their hands gently on their throats. First get them to

produce a long /h/ sound, then a long /ɑː/ sound (as in <u>ar</u>m) and to note the difference. They should feel a vibration in the throat with /ɑː/. Then ask them to repeat with the stop consonants practised here. They should feel little or no vibration in /k/, /t/ and /p/, and a noticeable vibration in /g/, /d/ and /b/.

3 *Answers*

Tom wants: some trousers, a tennis racket, a trumpet, a typewriter, a tent

Deborah wants: a dictionary, a desk, a dress, a dog

Kathy wants: a cat, a cake, a calendar, a clock, a camera

Gary wants: some gloves, a golf club

Pam wants: some perfume, a painting (or picture), a pen, a purse

Barbara wants: a blouse, a bracelet, a bookcase, a bicycle

Who wants most presents? *Tom*

Who wants fewest presents? *Gary*

In answer to 'Can you suggest some other presents they might like?', accept only words with a matching first letter.

In reporting back, monitor /p/, /b/, /t/, /d/, /k/ and /g/.

Extension

Go on to discuss other questions such as 'Who wants the best present(s)?', 'Who wants the most/least expensive present(s)?', 'Which present would *you* like best?' etc.

To give further practice, ask students to bring in small pictures from magazines of items that begin with these sounds. Stick them on a large piece of card and, at a later date, have students perform a similar task. You could adapt this task to practise almost any word-initial sounds that students find problematic.

4 The adjectives in box A and the nouns in box B all begin with the sounds practised in this unit. Target consonants are underlined.

<u>d</u>eep	<u>c</u>omfortable	<u>d</u>entist	<u>p</u>arty
<u>d</u>angerous	<u>p</u>atient	<u>d</u>octor	<u>p</u>ain
<u>g</u>ood	<u>t</u>errible	<u>g</u>arden	<u>t</u>iger
<u>b</u>eautiful		<u>b</u>ed	<u>t</u>elevision
<u>b</u>oring		<u>c</u>ave	<u>t</u>own
<u>b</u>ad		<u>c</u>amera	<u>t</u>eacher
<u>c</u>olourful		<u>c</u>ook	

Example answers

1 Something that is frightening: a deep cave, a dangerous tiger, a bad dentist

2 Something that is expensive: a good camera, a good television, a comfortable bed

3 Someone who does a good job: a good dentist/doctor/teacher/
cook, a patient dentist/doctor/teacher/cook
4 Someone who does not do a good job: a bad dentist/doctor/
teacher/cook
5 Something you like: a colourful garden, a good party,
a colourful town
6 Something you don't like: a terrible pain, a boring teacher

During repetition and reporting back, monitor the consonants
underlined in the words above.

Extension

You could adapt this task for better students. First ask for more example
words to go in either box A or B. Then ask pairs of students to write one
more appropriate 'Find someone/something …' instruction. When all
pairs have written at least one, list these on the board and ask students
to use the words presently in the boxes, together with the additional
words, to suggest answers.

Unit 11 /t/ & /d/ and /p/ & /b/

The four consonants practised in this unit are all stop consonants. The
first sounds in each pair (/t/ and /p/) are 'unvoiced' sounds; that is,
there is no vibration of the vocal folds when the sounds are made. The
second sounds in each pair (/d/ and /b/) are 'voiced' sounds. (See the
notes in Unit 10 suggesting how you can explain the difference to
students.)

Focus on /t/ and /d/

1 The words on the recording are:

1 president	2 pedestrian	3 midnight	4 introduce
5 industry	6 immediately	7 advertise	8 accident
9 granddaughter	10 stupid		

Answers

1 b	2 b	3 b	4 a	5 b
6 b	7 b	8 b	9 b	10 a

2 & 3 *Answers*

a) 1 & 9   b) 7 & 2   c) 5 & 3   d) 4 & 6   e) 10 & 8

3 During repetition and pairwork monitor the consonants /t/ and /d/.

Background

In 6, 8 and 10 some of the /t/ sounds will not be produced clearly when
the sentences are spoken at normal speed. For example, in 'It's ten pas(t)
ten' and 'I didn'(t)think…' the /t/ sounds circled will 'merge' with the next
consonant sound. You could point this out to better students and ask

them to say these sentences with the /t/ sounds changed in this way. More work on changes such as these will be found in Part 5, particularly Unit 40.

Focus on /p/ and /b/

4 The most likely answers are:
a piece of pie; a bottle of perfume; a pair of pyjamas; a book of stamps; a box of pencils; a portion of chips; a bag of shopping; a basket of pears; a plate of pasta; a packet of biscuits; a bunch of grapes; a pile of bricks; a bar of soap.

5 During repetition, monitor the pronunciation of /p/ and /b/.

6 When students report back their suggestions, monitor the pronunciation of /p/ and /b/. This could be given as a task for homework.

Unit 12 /s/, /z/, /f/, /v/, /θ/ and /ð/

> **Background**
> The consonants practised in this unit are sometimes referred to as 'fricative' consonants. In all of them, air is forced through a narrow gap at some point in the mouth to produce a hissing sound.

1 Monitor the pronunciation of the underlined consonants.

2 *Answers*
a) /f/ and /v/   b) /s/ and /z/   c) /θ/ and /ð/

See the notes in Unit 10 on the difference between voiced and unvoiced sounds. /z/, /v/ and /ð/ are voiced and /s/, /f/ and /θ/ are unvoiced.

3 In saying the numbers students will produce the target sounds for this unit. After pairwork, ask students to report back their decisions.
During pairwork and reporting back, monitor /s/, /z/, /f/, /v/, /θ/ and /ð/.

4 *Answers*

1 b	2 b	3 a	4 b	5 a	6 a	7 a	8 b
9 b	10 a	11 a	12 b	13 a	14 b	15 b	

5 In this task, students have to focus on the external features of sound production to be able to discriminate between the sounds. The idea is to make both 'hearer' and 'speaker' more aware of how the sounds are articulated, and differences between pairs of sounds.
Demonstrate what pairs need to do. Face the class and *silently* say either 'sat' or 'fat'. Ask them if you said word 1(a) or 1(b) in their book. Repeat until they clearly understand the task and then ask students to work in pairs.

Extension

For better students, write some imaginary newspaper headlines that include words with the consonants practised in Unit 12. For example:

FAULT IN THEATRE STARTS FIRE   FEWER IN SUMMER FLIGHT TO SUN

FIFTH SAILOR FOUND AT SEA   SECURITY SCARE ON FRENCH FERRY

VIOLENCE IN VILLAGE AFTER FOOTBALL

Ask students to work in pairs and to make up a brief story that might come after each headline. Then they tell their stories to the rest of the class. In discussion and reporting back, monitor the target consonants.

Unit 13 /θ/ & /ð/ and /v/, /f/ & /b/

Focus on /θ/ and /ð/

1 Monitor /θ/ and /ð/.

2 *Most likely answers*

1 A: Where's the toilet?
   B: The bathroom's through there.
   A: Thanks.
   B: That's OK.

2 A: What time's the train to Doncaster?
   B: Three thirty.
   A: When does it get there?
   B: Ten twenty-three.

3 A: Is that Tom and David?
   B: Yes, they're always together.
   A: They're brothers, aren't they?
   B: That's right.

Students should first work in pairs and say the conversations. Then nominate pairs to perform one of the conversations for the whole class. During pairwork and performance, monitor /θ/ and /ð/.

Extension

Ask students to find other words in their coursebooks that include the consonant pair 'th'. For each they should try to decide if it is pronounced /θ/ or /ð/.
   More practice of /θ/ and /ð/ can be found in Part 8, Unit 61.

Focus on /v/, /f/ and /b/

3 *Answers*

1 a   2 a   3 b   4 b   5 b   6 a   7 a   8 b
9 a   10 a

4 See the notes in Unit 12 for an explanation of this task. First demonstrate by facing the class and *silently* say either 'bone' or 'phone'. Ask them if you said word 1(a) or 1(b) in their book.

Repeat until they clearly understand the task and then ask students to work in pairs.

5 Point out the change that is needed to make questions from the statements in the column on the left. For the example, write on the board:

She watched television.   Where did Beverly watch television?

Most likely question and answer pairs are:

Where did Beverly ...

watch television?	In the living room.
buy some traveller's cheques?	In the bank (*or* At a travel agent's).
book a holiday?	At a travel agent's.
buy a novel?	From a bookshop.
deliver a birthday card?	To her neighbour.
have a very long bath?	In the bathroom.
borrow some books?	From the library.
have a conversation with a bus driver?	On a bus.
buy some bananas?	At a fruit and vegetable shop.

In pairwork and reporting back, monitor /v/, /f/ and /b/.

Unit 14 /ʃ/, /tʃ/, /ʒ/ and /dʒ/

> **Background**
>
> For the consonants practised in this unit, air is forced through a gap made between the front of the tongue and the top of the mouth, just behind the alveolar ridge which is the hard bony ridge behind the teeth. A hissing sound is produced as the air is forced through this gap. /ʃ/ and /ʒ/ are sometimes referred to as 'fricative' consonants. For the sounds /tʃ/ and /dʒ/ there is a complete closure of the gap and a slight build up of pressure before the air is forced through the gap. These are sometimes referred to as 'affricate' (pronounced /'æfrɪkət/) consonants. /ʃ/ and /tʃ/ are unvoiced, and /ʒ/ and /dʒ/ are voiced sounds.

1 Monitor the underlined consonants.

2 *Most likely answers*

a) watch television?	In the lounge.
b) arrange a holiday?	At a travel agent's.
c) buy shoes?	At a shoe shop.
d) wash up?	In the kitchen.
e) keep cheese?	In the fridge.
f) learn a foreign language?	At college.
g) catch a coach?	At a coach station.

h) cash a cheque? At a bank.
i) buy matches? At a newsagent's.
j) keep a car? In the garage.

During pairwork monitor /ʃ/, /tʃ/, /ʒ/ and /dʒ/.

3 & 4 During repetition and pairwork monitor /ʃ/, /tʃ/, /ʒ/ and /dʒ/.

5 The food and drink from the box in **3** that appear in the conversation are:

sugar   chips   chocolate   fish   fresh vegetables
porridge

The students should place a tick next to these words.

On the recording:

P(atient): So how much do I have to lose, then?

D(octor): Well, Mr Taylor, I would suggest at least two stone.

P: Oh dear. How could I do that?

D: Well, let's look at what you're eating at the moment, shall we? Give me an idea of what sort of things you eat during the day.

P: Well, I've got a very sweet tooth, I'm afraid. I eat a lot of sugar. I like chips a lot and I'm addicted to chocolate. I have to have a lot of chocolate.

D: I see.

P: Is that wrong?

D: Well, yes it is. I'm going to give you a diet sheet, and I recommend that you follow it. The most important things to put into your diet are fish, fresh vegetables and something like porridge for breakfast.

P: Oh, porridge. I like porridge.

D: Good.

P: Can I make it with milk…?

6 During pairwork monitor the /ʃ/, /tʃ/, /ʒ/ and /dʒ/ sounds in the words from the box in **3**.

> **Extension**
>
> Ask students to look through the words in the unit that include the sounds /ʃ/, /tʃ/, /ʒ/ and /dʒ/ and find out how many ways they can find of spelling each of these sounds.
> /ʃ/ can be spelt 's' (e.g. sugar); 'sh' (short); 'ch' (champagne); 't' (station).
> /tʃ/ can be spelt 'ch' (chair); 'tch' (kitchen).
> /ʒ/ can be spelt 's' (decision); 'g' (garage).
> /dʒ/ can be spelt 'g' (general); 'j' (June); 'dg' (porridge).
>
> There is more on the spelling of /ʃ/ and /tʃ/ in the next unit. See also Part 8, Unit 62.

Unit 15 /ʃ/ & /tʃ/ and /dr/ & /tr/

Focus *on /ʃ/ and /tʃ/*

1 *Answers*

	/ʃ/	/tʃ/		/ʃ/	/tʃ/
information	☑	☐	special	☑	☐
furniture	☐	☑	commercial	☑	☐
education	☑	☐	temperature	☐	☑
insurance	☑	☐	examination	☑	☐
suggestion	☐	☑	picture	☐	☑
profession	☑	☐	delicious	☑	☐
question	☐	☑	station	☑	☐

2 Before repeating and checking, rewind the recording. During repetition, monitor /ʃ/ and /tʃ/.

Focus *on /dr/ and /tr/*

3 In some of these words, /tr/ is part of a longer series of consonants (e.g. /str/ in street, Austria, instruments, Australia, pedestrians; and /ntr/ in countries). /tr/ often occurs in longer 'consonant clusters' such as these, so examples are included in this task. More work on consonant clusters is found in Part 3.

Monitor /dr/ and /tr/ in these words.

4 *Answers*
1 A: It's a really busy *street*.
   B: Yes, there's always a lot of *traffic* and *pedestrians*.
2 A: Which *instruments* do you play?
   B: The *trumpet* and the *drums*.
3 A: What *countries* would you most like to visit?
   B: *Australia* and *Austria*.
4 A: Are you going to *drive*?
   B: No, I'll *travel* by *train*.
5 A: Is her *dress dry* yet?
   B: Yes, it's in the *wardrobe*.

During pairwork monitor /dr/ and /tr/.

> **Extension**
>
> Ask students to work in pairs to collect more words including /dr/ and /tr/ from their coursebooks. They should try to write similar two-line conversations including the words and say them for the rest of the class. Monitor the pronunciation of /dr/ and /tr/ as they do so. Make a note of the conversations they have written and use them to practise these sounds at a later date.

Unit 16 /w/, /r/, /j/ and /l/

Background
The sounds practised in Units 16, 17 and 18 (/w/, /r/, /j/, /l/, /m/, /n/ and /ŋ/) are sometimes referred to as 'approximants'. These sounds are consonants, but are produced without the complete closure of the stop consonants or the audible hiss of the fricative or affricate consonants practised in earlier units in Part 2.

1 Monitor the underlined consonants.

2 /w/ sounds are underlined. The 'w' letter that is not pronounced /w/ is circled.

A: <u>Wh</u>at's the <u>w</u>eather like?　　A: Shall <u>we</u> have a <u>w</u>alk any<u>w</u>ay?

B: Aⓦful. It's <u>w</u>et and <u>w</u>indy.　　B: Let's <u>w</u>ait t<u>w</u>enty minutes.

During repetition and pairwork, monitor /w/.

3 /j/ sounds are underlined. The 'y' letters that are not pronounced /j/ are circled. The /j/ sounds not written with the letter 'y' are marked.

　　　　　　　　　　/j/
A: I had an interview <u>y</u>esterdaⓨ.
B: Where?　　　　　↑
　　　　　　　　　　/j/
A: At the Dailⓨ News.
　　　　　　　↑
B: Did <u>y</u>ou get the job?
A: I don't know <u>y</u>et.

During repetition and pairwork, monitor /j/.

4 /r/ sounds are underlined. The 'r' letters that are not pronounced /r/ are circled.

A: Did you <u>r</u>ememberⓡ to <u>r</u>ing <u>R</u>ay?

B: I <u>tr</u>ied th<u>r</u>ee times on <u>Fr</u>iday.

A: He was p<u>r</u>obably at woⓡk.

B: You'ⓡe p<u>r</u>obably <u>r</u>ight. I'll <u>tr</u>y again tomo<u>rr</u>ow.

During repetition and pairwork, monitor /r/.

Background
Different accents of English differ in how they treat the letter 'r' when:
a) it is followed by a consonant letter, e.g. in the word 'a<u>r</u>m';
b) it is followed by a silent letter 'e', e.g. in the word 'ca<u>r</u>e';
c) it occurs at the end of a word, e.g. 'docto<u>r</u>'.
In most varieties of the English spoken in England and Australia the letter 'r' in these positions is *not* pronounced. These accents are sometimes referred to as 'non-rhotic' accents. In General American and the English

spoken in Ireland and Scoland, for example, this 'r' *is* pronounced. These accents are often referred to as 'rhotic' accents.

In this book, the model of pronunciation used is Southern British English, a non-rhotic accent. If your students are likely to have contact with speakers of a rhotic accent of English, point this out to them. If possible, let them listen to tape recordings of rhotic accents and point out instances in which 'r' is pronounced where it would be silent in a non-rhotic accent.

5 Conversation on the recording:

BOB: Hello, Sarah.

SARAH: Hi, Bob.

B: You've been away, haven't you?

S: Yeah, I've had a lovely holiday. I went to Sweden.

B: Oh, great. Did you go on your own or...

S: No. I went with somebody I work with, a friend, yeah.

B: Fantastic. Where did you stay?

S: Well, it was in a very small place. I stayed in a small hotel. It was, you know, nothing luxurious, but it was clean and it was quiet.

B: Sounds great.

S: Yeah, it was lovely.

B: What did you get up to? Was there much to do out there?

S: Well, it's very sporty. We did a lot of swimming, and I tried windsurfing.

B: Oh, I've always wanted to do that.

S: Yeah, it's good.

B: Must have been good weather then?

S: Well, it wasn't very warm, but no, it was quite cool, but we were lucky it didn't rain. No, it was dry all the time.

B: Oh, great, you're looking fantastic.

Spaces in column A to be completed as follows:

Where?	Sweden
Who with?	with a friend
Hotel?	clean, quiet
Things to do?	windsurfing, swimming
Weather?	cool, dry

6 Pairwork can be followed by performance by selected pairs. Monitor the target sounds /w/, /r/, /j/ and /l/ underlined in the words below.

Where?	Ita<u>l</u>y, Bu<u>lga</u>ria, the <u>U</u>SA, S<u>w</u>eden
Who with?	<u>w</u>ith fami<u>l</u>y, a<u>l</u>one, <u>w</u>ith a <u>fr</u>iend
Hotel?	c<u>l</u>ean, comfortab<u>l</u>e, s<u>w</u>imming poo<u>l</u>, <u>l</u>arge, o<u>l</u>d, q<u>u</u>iet , uncomfortab<u>l</u>e
Things to do?	s<u>w</u>imming, <u>w</u>alking, <u>y</u>achting, <u>w</u>indsurfing, s<u>l</u>eeping, fi<u>l</u>ms

Weather?   lovely, cloudy, <u>w</u>et, coo<u>l</u>, <u>w</u>indy, d<u>r</u>y, usua<u>ll</u>y
hot, co<u>l</u>d

Unit 17   /w/ & /v/ and /r/ & /l/

Focus on /w/ and /v/

1 *Answers*
    1   2   I'<u>ve</u> only got twel<u>ve</u>.
    2   1   She works hard e<u>v</u>ery day.
    3   3   We had to dri<u>v</u>e up the pa<u>v</u>ement to a<u>v</u>oid him.
    4   3   I'<u>ve</u> lost my wallet, tra<u>v</u>eller's cheques and <u>v</u>isa.
    5   3   We're ha<u>v</u>ing <u>v</u>isitors o<u>v</u>er the weekend.

2 Before checking and repeating, rewind the recording. During
repetition, monitor /v/.

3 *Answers*
    1   2   <u>W</u>hat's this <u>o</u>ne over here?
    2   2   <u>W</u>as every piece of furniture made of <u>w</u>ood?
    3   2   It's q<u>u</u>ite <u>w</u>arm for November.
    4   3   They're having just a q<u>u</u>iet <u>w</u>edding next <u>W</u>ednesday.
    5   4   It <u>w</u>as very <u>w</u>et last <u>w</u>eek, <u>w</u>asn't it?

4 Before checking and repeating, rewind the recording. During
repetition, monitor /w/.

Focus on /r/ and /l/

5 *Possible answers*
You might say...	but probably not...
a rich uncle	a rich letter
a slippery road	a slippery river
a musical instrument	a musical football
an electronic calculator	an electronic letter
a horrible brother	a horrible river
a dangerous road	a dangerous calculator
a difficult problem	a difficult bathroom
Australian football	an Australian bathroom
a clean bathroom	a clean uncle
a private road	a private flower
a lovely flower	a lovely problem
a favourite building	a favourite calculator

During pairwork and reporting back, monitor /r/ and /l/.

> **Extension**
> You could adapt this task to provide practice of other pairs of
> consonants or vowels.

Unit 18 /m/, /n/ and /ŋ/

> **Background**
>
> The three sounds practised in this unit are often referred to as 'nasal' consonants because the air is pushed out of the nose. Notice that the sound /ŋ/ does not occur at the beginning of English words, but is found between vowels and also very frequently at the end of words.

1 Monitor the pronunciation of the underlined consonants.

2 *Answers*

1 He's ironing.
2 He's listening to music.
3 He's painting.
4 He's studying English grammar.
5 He's shopping.
6 He's singing.
7 He's washing up.
8 He's cooking.
9 He's gardening.
10 He's playing tennis.

During repetition monitor the pronunciation of the underlined consonants.

3 *Answers*

1 He likes ironing.
2 He doesn't like listening to music.
3 He likes painting.
4 He likes studying English grammar.
5 He doesn't like shopping.
6 He likes singing.
7 He doesn't like washing up.
8 He likes cooking.
9 He likes gardening.
10 He doesn't like playing tennis.

During pairwork monitor the pronunciation of the underlined consonants.

> **Extension**
>
> Students work in pairs and ask each other whether they like or dislike doing these things. Monitor the target consonants while they report what they have found to the class. Substitute other verbs for more variety.

4 During pairwork and reporting back monitor the pronunciation of the target consonants in the words in the lists. They are underlined here:

Arrange visa for holiday in India.
Get money.
Do shopping. Buy handbag, perfume, sunglasses, computer magazine.
See new James Bond film.
Have dinner with Norma.

cinema   bank
supermarket   chemist
department store
newsagent   restaurant
Indian Embassy

Part 3 Consonant clusters

UNITS 19–26

Aims and organisation

In Part 3 students practise **consonant clusters** at the beginning of words, at the end of words and at word boundaries.

Unit 19
Distinguishes between consonant **letters** and consonant **sounds,** and introduces the idea of a consonant cluster.

Unit 20
Consonant clusters at the beginning of words.

Unit 21
More on consonant clusters at the beginning of words.

Unit 22
Consonant clusters at the end of words.

Unit 23
More on consonant clusters at the end of words.

Unit 24
Consonant clusters in the middle of words.

Unit 25
Consonant clusters that occur across word boundaries.

Unit 26
More on consonant clusters that occur across word boundaries.

General notes

A **consonant cluster** occurs when two or more **consonant sounds** are said without an intervening vowel sound. Notice that a consonant cluster isn't always found where there are two written consonant letters: for example, the word 'shop' begins with two consonant letters, but only one consonant sound.

Background

Different languages allow different possible combinations of consonants in clusters. So, for example, /gd/ is not a possible cluster at the beginning of an English word.

Consonant clusters that are possible in some positions in words are not possible in other positions. For example, /ts/ is possible at the end of an English word (e.g. hats), but not at the beginning. For details of possible consonant clusters at word beginnings and ends in English, see Gimson (1989, pp. 243-56) in the list of *Recommended books* on page 3. Notice that the range of possible clusters in the middle of words and across word boundaries is much greater than those possible at the beginning and end of single words.

Notes on each unit

Unit 19 Consonant letters and consonant sounds

1 This introduces the idea of a consonant cluster. To check that students have understood, write words on the board that include consonant clusters at the beginning, at the end, and somewhere in the middle. Select students to come to the board to underline the consonant clusters in each word. Point out, too, that consonant clusters can occur across word boundaries. Write up, for example, 'roof top' and 'call me' and underline like this:

'roo<u>f t</u>op'   'ca<u>ll m</u>e'

to show the consonant clusters.

2 *Answers*

	Number of consonant letters	Number of consonant sounds		Number of consonant letters	Number of consonant sounds
1 <u>bl</u>ood	2	2 (/bl/)	7 ligh<u>t</u>	3	1 (/t/)
2 ju<u>mp</u>	2	2 (/mp/)	8 ne<u>xt</u>	2	3 (/kst/)
3 ti<u>ck</u>et	2	1 (/k/)	9 <u>th</u>ere	2	1 (/ð/)
4 ta<u>bl</u>et	2	2 (/bl/)	10 repor<u>t</u>	2	1 (/t/)
5 do<u>ll</u>ar	2	1 (/l/)	11 fi<u>lm</u>	2	2 (/lm/)
6 <u>ch</u>air	2	1 (/tʃ/)	12 <u>str</u>eet	3	3 (/str/)

Draw attention to the fact that the number of consonant *sounds* may differ from the number of consonant *letters*.

3 *Possible answers* Take other suggestions from students.

	/l/	/m/	/r/
/k/	clock	✗	cross
/d/	✗	✗	dress
/g/	glass	✗	grapes
/p/	plug	✗	prize
/s/	slow	small	✗
/t/	✗	✗	triangle

Background

Note that 'Sri' in 'Sri Lanka' is the only word beginning with 'sr' that is regularly used in English.

4 If students identify that they have particular problems, ask them to consider why this might be. It is probably most likely that the consonant cluster doesn't occur in their own language, although it isn't always the case that consonant clusters that don't occur in the native language cause difficulties when they occur in English. You might like to make a note for future work of difficulties that students say they have.

5 This is a 'round-the-class' activity. Point out that *one* of the consonant sounds is repeated in the consonant cluster beginning successive words. For the chain given here, for example, we have:

/bl/   /br/   /kr/   /kl/   /sl/   /st/   /sp/   /pl/

To check that students have understood, ask for suggestions on how the chain given in the book might continue. Start a new chain by giving a word yourself and asking for a suggestion for the next word. Continue to ask for suggestions as the chain grows, or nominate students. Wrong words or repetitions mean elimination. Keep a note of words that cause problems and at the end check that students can pronounce them correctly.

Unit 20 Consonant clusters at the beginning of words

1 & 4 Monitor the underlined consonant clusters. Make a note of which clusters cause problems for which students. Not all will be difficult for all students.

Use (1) to (7) in **1** and (8) to (12) in **4** as 'practice lists'. Refer students back to them if they have particular problems of pronouncing word-initial consonant clusters in the future.

Extension

The consonant clusters practised in these lists are among the most common in English, but many others are possible. If you notice that your students have problems with a cluster not given in (1)–(12) write your own list of words beginning with the problem cluster. Perhaps pin a large version of it on a wall and have students repeat the words on the list each time they make a mistake in pronouncing the cluster.

2 Monitor the consonant clusters underlined in **3** below.

3 *Answers*

What did Sue have for Christmas?	A <u>bl</u>ue <u>bl</u>ouse.
How can I speak English better?	<u>Pr</u>actise your <u>pr</u>onunciation.
What do we need from the supermarket?	Just <u>br</u>ead and <u>cr</u>isps.
What should I take on my holiday to Iceland?	<u>Pl</u>enty of warm <u>cl</u>othes.
What's the weather like?	<u>Qu</u>ite <u>cl</u>oudy.

During pairwork, monitor the consonant clusters underlined.

5 *Answers*

How many tickets do you want?	<u>Thr</u>ee, <u>pl</u>ease.
Where shall we meet?	At the <u>br</u>idge by the <u>st</u>ation.
What do you like best on TV?	<u>Thr</u>illers and <u>sp</u>orts <u>pr</u>ogrammes.
What did you buy in town?	A <u>cl</u>ock and some new <u>tr</u>ousers.
Oh, no, I've missed it.	It's OK. There are <u>pl</u>enty more <u>tr</u>ains this evening.
He can't understand my English.	<u>Tr</u>y <u>sp</u>eaking more <u>sl</u>owly.

6 During pairwork, monitor the consonant clusters underlined in **5** above.

Unit 21 More on consonant clusters at the beginning of words

1 Students have to discriminate between words that begin with a consonant cluster and words that begin with a single consonant sound.

Answers
1 Is the <u>cl</u>ock broken?
2 They'll <u>gr</u>ow much higher than that.
3 He used to be a postman, but now he's a <u>d</u>iver.
4 Shall we <u>p</u>ay now or later?
5 How much money did she <u>sp</u>end?
6 How many have you <u>b</u>ought?

7 The <u>plane</u> was terrible.

8 Are you sure it's <u>true</u>?

9 Did you <u>say</u> two weeks or three?

10 What <u>sport</u> do you like best?

2 You may want to demonstrate this first. Say, for example, 'Is the lock broken?' and ask students if you are including a word from box A or B. Then students work in pairs.

3 Before repeating the words, check that students understand them by asking them to write the words next to the pictures.

Answers

1 a dress   2 a frying pan   3 flippers   4 a swimming costume   5 gloves   6 a clock   7 a sweater
8 a sleeping bag   9 a scarf   10 a ski suit   11 swimming trunks   12 skis   13 a plate   14 a spade   15 slippers

4 On the recording:

A: Oh, Andrew.

B: Hello.

A: I wanted to ask you a couple of questions. I'm going on holiday skiing soon and I wanted to ask you what you think I should take. Obviously, I've got to take a ski suit and gloves.

B: Yes, you'll need gloves. You'll definitely need those. If you've got your own skis, too, that could save you a lot of money because otherwise you have to hire them and it's quite expensive. Where are you going to stay?

A: Oh, I'm staying in a hotel. Quite a big one, I think.

B: Well in that case I should take your swimming costume because most of these big hotels they have indoor pools nowadays...

A: That's a good idea.

B: ...it's really relaxing, you know, having a swim after skiing all day.

A: Andrew, do you think I'll be warm enough in a ski suit? I mean, without a jacket on top?

B: I should think so, yes. I mean, if you've got your ski suit and a couple of warm sweaters, and a scarf perhaps. Yeah, you should be OK with that.

A: So no jacket...

Students should place a tick next to: swimming costume, gloves, sweater, scarf, ski suit, skis.

5 You may want to demonstrate **5** with a good student before you ask students to work in pairs. Use some of the phrases given in the book during your demonstration. Talk about as many of the items in the pictures as you can. While students make similar conversations, monitor the consonant clusters in the words in the pictures.

Extension

At a later date, do a similar exercise which focuses on particular problems you have noticed some or all of your students have. For example, if you have noticed that some of your students have difficulties pronouncing words beginning 'br' and 'bl' (for example, they might pronounce the beginning of the word 'brown' as /bər/ or /əbr/) make a list of a number of things beginning with these sounds (e.g. bread, a broom, a blanket, a blouse) and ask them to discuss which they would buy for a present for a son/daughter/mother etc., or which they would usually find in the kitchen/bedroom, etc. Monitor the target consonant clusters.

Unit 22 Consonant clusters at the end of words

1 When you are playing the recording, pause after each word to allow students time to think and to write down their answers.

2 Rewind and repeat.

Answers

/n/ + /s/	/n/ + /t/	/n/ + /d/
since	want	friend
silence	haven't	understand
pronounce	important	thousand
once	different	find

When students repeat the words, monitor the final consonant clusters.

3 *Answers*

How long have you been here?   <u>Since</u> Wednesday.
Do you <u>want</u> one?   No, thanks.
Aren't they the same?   No, they're <u>different</u>.
How often do you come?   <u>Once</u> a week.
Is this your sister?   No, my <u>friend</u>.
You've taken my coat!   No, I <u>haven't</u>.

4 Monitor the final consonant clusters.

5 *Likely answers*

Things you can eat or drink: toast, beans, orange, milk, chips
Animals: elephant, beetle, wasp, fox, ant
Parts of the body: waist, ankle, wrist, tongue, chest
People: adult, child, yourself, parents, boyfriend
Ways people feel: pleased, terrible, amused, depressed

6 One student from each pair should report back. From the first pair ask for 'things you can eat or drink', from the second 'animals', etc.
During repetition and reporting back, monitor final consonant clusters.

Extension

For homework, ask students to collect three words they know (these could be taken from their coursebook, for example) that end in a consonant cluster. These three words should have some connection (e.g. all found in the home). Discourage plurals which often end in a consonant + 's'. Students should report these in class. Collect their answers and use them to do a similar task to that in **4** to **6** at a later date.

Unit 23 More on consonant clusters at the end of words

Background

Most syllables contain a vowel. Some words, though, like 'trouble' (/trʌbl̩/) and 'listen' (/lɪsn̩/) will usually be thought of as having two syllables, with the final syllable consisting only of the last consonant. These consonants that sound like syllables are often referred to as 'syllabic consonants', and are the focus of tasks **1** to **4** in this unit. /l/ and /n/ are by far the most common syllabic consonants, especially in Southern British English.

   Instead of a syllabic consonant it is always possible to produce an ordinary consonant cluster with the vowel /ə/ (for example, /trʌbəl/ or /lɪsən/) although native speakers will generally pronounce this as a very short vowel. Learners of English often tend to make this vowel too long and this should be discouraged.

1 Students may tend to insert a full vowel sound between the last two consonants. Point out that although the words end in consonant clusters, a *very short* vowel sound may occur between the consonants. Monitor and correct students if they produce anything longer than a very short vowel sound inside the consonant cluster.

2 & 3 *Answers*

1 A: Where's your <u>cousin</u>?
   B: She's in <u>hospital</u>.
   A: What's the <u>trouble</u>?
   B: She fell off her <u>bicycle</u>.

2 A: When's the <u>examination</u>?
   B: At <u>eleven</u>.
   A: How do you feel?
   B: <u>Terrible</u>.

3 A: What's in this <u>bottle</u>?
   B: A <u>chemical</u>.
   A: What's it for?
   B: Something <u>special</u>!

4 A: Press that <u>button</u>.
   B: This one in the <u>middle</u>?
   A: Yes.
   B: What'll <u>happen</u>?
   A: Just <u>listen</u>.

4 Rewind and repeat. During repetition and pairwork, monitor the final consonant clusters.

5 & 6 If possible, students should interview a number of people and note their answers. In the reporting back stage they can make statements like: 'Most people I talked to liked physics best at school,' 'Nobody I spoke to wanted to be a politician.'

When students report back, monitor the final consonant clusters.

Unit 24 Consonant clusters in the middle of words

1 This is perhaps best done in pairs, if possible with students having different first languages. Ask them to complete the column on the left first, check the answers, and then do the column on the right. The words given below are suggestions only.

Beginning	Middle	End
✓ stop	cus<u>t</u>omer	✓ last
✗	seve<u>nt</u>een	✓ went
✗	Dece<u>mb</u>er	✗ [1]
✗	shou<u>ld</u>er	✓ old
✓ prize	A<u>pr</u>il	✗
✗	co<u>mp</u>any	✓ lump
✗	bla<u>nk</u>et	✓ bank
✗	e<u>nv</u>elope	✗

[1] Notice that some words end with the consonant *letters* 'mb' (for example, 'lamb'), but no English words end with the consonant *sounds* /mb/.

2 Students repeat after the recording. Point out after the exercise that:

a) 'x' in 'exercise' and in 'taxi' is a consonant cluster /ks/ even though it is only one consonant letter;

b) 'p' in 'raspberry' is not pronounced;

c) 'e' in 'advertis<u>e</u>ment' is not pronounced.

Monitor the underlined consonant clusters.

3 Point out that what is given on the left represents sounds and not letters. So, for example, /zb/ in number 5 may not necessarily be written with the letters 'zb'. In doing this exercise, students have to decide what words in the box in **2** contain the sounds given (there are two in each case) and which of these are appropriate. Alternatively, they may look for words that fit the context (at least two of the words fit each context) and decide which of these contains the required sound.

Answers

1 passport   2 loudly   3 taxi   4 quietly   5 husband
6 painting   7 businessman   8 doctor   9 aeroplane
10 boyfriend

Ask students to report their answers to the class. Monitor consonant clusters.

4 Monitor consonant clusters.

5 *Answers*
1 Cities: Oslo, Bombay, London
2 Months: April, December, October
3 Pieces of furniture: wardrobe, armchair, bookshelf
4 Things to eat: apple pie, chocolates, biscuits, cornflakes
5 Things that use electricity: toaster, tape recorder, computer
6 Buildings: library, hospital, post office, bookshop

6 Monitor consonant clusters.

Unit 25 Consonant clusters across words

1 *Answers*
orange juice, arrival time, capital city, classical music, film star, girlfriend, left-handed, portable television

2 Monitor the consonant clusters at the word boundaries.

3 During repetition, monitor the consonant clusters at the word boundaries.

4 *Answers*
1 (b) (People talking about some photographs one of them has taken).
2 (d) (Students talking about their homework)
3 (a) (People talking about a pop concert)
4 (c) (People talking about a missing car)

5 During pairwork, monitor the consonant clusters at the word boundaries.

> **Extension**
>
> Take a section from a conversation given in the students' coursebook. Ask them to first underline consonant clusters they expect to hear across word boundaries. Then play the accompanying recording and note how these clusters are pronounced. The students repeat after the recording. Monitor the clusters they have underlined.

Unit 26 More on consonant clusters across words

1 & 2 During repetition and pairwork, monitor the lengthening of the consonant at the word boundaries.

2 *Answers*
She was wearing her red dress at the party.
We lost the match one nil.
Five visitors came to see us yesterday.

They had a team meeting after the game.
Is there enough food for the party?
A bad dream woke me up.
There's some money in my purse.
It takes five minutes.

3

> ### Background
>
> The near or complete omission of the /t/ or /d/ sounds at the end of words very often occurs in speech produced at normal speed. It most frequently occurs when /t/ or /d/ are followed by a word beginning with a consonant and when /t/ is preceded by /f/ or /s/, and when /d/ is preceded by /l/ or /n/. For example:
>
> left luggage, last Saturday, cold nose, sand castle.
>
> Further information and practice on changes such as these can be found in Part 5.

4 *Answers*

1 cold	2 pleased	3 that	4 contact	5 fact
6 visit	7 friend	8 can't		

5 Rewind and repeat. During repetition, monitor the changes in pronunciation in the consonant clusters at the word boundaries.

6 *Answers*

1 That's true.
2 I don't know yet.
3 Help yourself.
4 It's very pretty.
5 Please try.

6 Can you come tomorrow?
7 Can I have some more?
8 Thanks very much.
9 But it's so expensive.

7 *Most likely answers*

a) 4, 9, 1
b) 6, 2, 5
c) 7, 3, 8

During pairwork, monitor the consonant clusters underlined in **6** above.

Part 4 Stress and rhythm

Aims and organisation

In Part 4 students learn about **syllables** in words, the pronunciation of **stressed** and **unstressed** syllables, and the **rhythm** of spoken English.

Unit 27
Syllables, stressed syllables and unstressed syllables.

Unit 28
Identifying stressed syllables and patterns of stressed and unstressed syllables.

Unit 29
More on patterns of stressed and unstressed syllables. Focus on stress patterns in numbers.

Unit 30
A simple rule to predict stress in English nouns, verbs and adjectives. Understanding the information about stress given in dictionaries.

Unit 31
Unstressed syllables that include the vowel sound /ə/.

Unit 32
The stressed and unstressed forms of 'of', 'to' and 'and', and their importance in producing an English rhythm.

Unit 33
More on rhythm in sentences.

Unit 34
Moving stress in longer words. Focus on nationalities and numbers.

General notes

Background
A **syllable** is a group of sounds that are pronounced together. Syllables always contain a vowel, except in the case of syllabic consonants (see the notes to Unit 23). This vowel may be preceded by one or more consonants and may be followed by one or more consonants.

When a word is said on its own its syllables will be either **stressed** or **unstressed**. Here are some examples of words showing stressed (marked O over the vowel) and unstressed (marked o) syllables:

O   o O   o   O o

farm   be-gin   com-put-er

Some words have two kinds of stressed syllable: a **primary stressed syllable** and a **secondary stressed syllable**. For example, in the word 'guarantee' the last syllable has primary stress, the first has secondary stress and the middle syllable is unstressed. In dictionaries the primary and secondary stressed syllables are usually indicated like this:

guarantee /ˌgærənˈtiː/

Some dictionaries show a third kind of stress, tertiary stress, but this is not very important in learning about the pronunciation of English words.

The importance of knowing about stress in words in isolation in speaking English is talked about more in the general notes for Part 6.

The **rhythm** of English is largely concerned with patterns of stressed and unstressed syllables and how the pronunciation of certain words is different in their stressed and unstressed forms.

Notes on each unit

Unit 27 Syllables and stress

1 & 2 This task introduces the idea that words can be divided into syllables.

2 *Answers*

furniture 3   bought 1   blackboard 2   examination 5
remember 3   collect 2   anybody 4   please 1
grandmother 3   impossible 4   electricity 5   rabbit 2
directions 3   goodbye 2

3

Extension

If the students share a language in which only one syllable in a word is normally stressed, list a few words in that language with more than one syllable and ask them to say where the stress is in each. If the students share a language like Japanese in which syllables normally carry equal stress, list some words and phrases in that language to show that stress operates differently from the way it does in English.

If you write down new words for students to copy and learn, mark the word stress in this way. Encourage students to learn the stress when they revise the words.

Answers

○ ○○   ○   ○   ○   ○ ○ ○○ ○
furniture   bought   blackboard   examination

○ ○ ○   ○ ○   ○ ○ ○ ○   ○   ○   ○ ○
remember   collect   anybody   please   grandmother

○ ○ ○ ○   ○ ○ ○○ ○   ○ ○   ○ ○ ○   ○ ○
impossible   electricity   rabbit   directions   goodbye

4 Rewind and repeat. During repetition, monitor stress placement.

5 *Answers*

○ ○ ○   ○ ○   ○ ○   ○ ○   ○ ○ ○   ○ ○
Budapest   Bangkok   Madrid   Moscow   Jakarta   Lima

To check answers, write the names of the cities on the board. Ask
students to come to the front and draw circles over the names.

> **Extension**
>
> You could develop this activity by asking for more capital cities – and
> giving the names in English if the students don't know them. If you
> think it is appropriate for your students, use this opportunity to show
> that it is sometimes difficult to decide how many syllables a word has
> got. For example, 'Tokyo' when said slowly, would probably have three
> syllables, To-ky-o, but if said quickly probably only two, To-kyo. The
> same is true for cities such as Canberra and Brasilia.
>
> If students have multisyllabic names with stressed and unstressed
> syllables, write some of them on the board. Ask other students to come
> and draw large and small circles over the names to indicate stressed and
> unstressed syllables.

Unit 28 Patterns of stress in words

1 The odd one out in each list is:

   ○ ○   ○ ○   ○ ○ ○   ○○ ○
1 chicken   2 Japan   3 telephone   4 policeman

   ○ ○   ○ ○
5 supermarket

2 Monitor stress placement.

> **Extension**
>
> You could give students a simple rule that helps explain stress in some of
> the words in this task. Ask students what they notice about stress in the
> words *injection, competition, information* and *immigration*. The stressed
> syllable is the one before the *-ion* ending. Most words that end with *-ion*
> have stress in this position, irrespective of stress in the 'base' form (that
> is, the word without *-ion*). Demonstrate this with:

○ ○　　○ ○　○　　　　　○ ○　　　○　○　　○ ○
inject – injection　　　　inform – information
　○　　○　　　○　　○○○　　○　○　○　　　○　　○　○○
compete – competition　immigrate – immigration

Ask better students to collect more words ending with *-ion* and find out if the rule works for these.

3 *Answers*

　○　○　　　○ ○
A single or return?

　　○　○　　　　　　○ ○
I'm a stranger here myself.

　　　○ ○　　　○　○
Have you ever been abroad?

　　　○○　　　○　○
Is the station far away?

　　　　○ ○　　　○ ○
I was hoping to invite you.

　　　○ ○　　　○ ○
I'll be busy, I'm afraid.

　　　○ ○　　　　○ ○
I'd like a ticket to Madrid.

　　　○○　　○ ○　○
I went to Brazil in April.

In repetition, monitor stress on the two-syllable words.

4 *Best answers*

I'd like a ticket to Madrid.　A single or return?
Is the station far away?　　　I'm a stranger here myself.
I was hoping to invite you.　I'll be busy, I'm afraid.
Have you ever been abroad?　I went to Brazil in April.

In pairwork, monitor stress on the two-syllable words.

Unit 29 More practice; stress patterns in numbers

1 *Answers*

economics 4　　Zimbabwe 3　　diplomat 3　　July 2
Chinese 2　　biology 4　　Arabic 3　　Peru 2　　August 2
photographer 4　　Norwegian 3　　Germany 3　　accountant 3
chemistry 3　　September 3

During repetition, monitor stress in the words.

2 *Answers*

1 accountant　　2 August　　3 biology　　4 Norwegian
5 Zimbabwe

Monitor stress in these words.

3 *Answers*

1 11.14　　2 50　　3 16　　4 17　　5 £2.80　　6 £90

The sentences on the recording are:
1 The next train to arrive at this platform is the 11.14 to Birmingham.
2 I've got a very old car. It can only go at 50 kilometres per hour.

3 We could meet in my office. It's number 16.

4 My brother is 35, but his wife is 17!

5 It's very good, and it only cost £2.80.

6 I once stayed in a hotel in London which cost £90 a night.

To check the answers write the pairs of numbers on the board and point to one as the students say their answers. That way you can make sure *they* are saying them correctly.

5 Rewind and repeat. Pause the recording at the end of each line for repetition. Monitor stress in the numbers.

6 Monitor stress in the numbers.

> **Extension**
>
> 'Bingo!' Write the numbers 13, 14, 15, 16, 17, 18, 19, 30, 40, 50, 60, 70, 80 and 90 on the board. Tell students to write down four of them. Then say the numbers slowly at random. Keep a note yourself of which ones you have said. Students should cross out the numbers as they hear you say them. When they have crossed out all four they should shout 'Bingo!' and they have won the game – if they have heard you correctly, of course. Ask the winner to read out his or her four numbers while you check that you said them. After a few games like this, ask a student to take on the role of 'caller'.

Unit 30 Finding out about stress patterns

1 Explain that although word stress in English is 'mobile', that is, it does not go on the same syllable in every word, it is possible to see some general patterns. Understanding these can help students predict where stress goes in new words they meet.

If necessary, remind students about the meaning of 'noun', 'verb' and 'adjective'. Ask them to write N (for noun), V (for verb) or A (for adjective) next to the words.

Answers

carry (V)	famous (A)	daughter (N)	husband (N)
forget (V)	lovely (A)	yellow (A)	prefer (V)
frighten (V)	kitchen (N)	ugly (A)	mountain (N)

2 *Answers*

O o	O o	O o	O o	o O	O o
carry	famous	daughter	husband	forget	lovely

O o	o O	O o	O o	O o	O o
yellow	prefer	frighten	kitchen	ugly	mountain

3 Most <u>nouns</u> and <u>adjectives</u> are stressed on the first syllable. Some <u>verbs</u> are stressed on the first syllable and others on the second.

4 *Answers*

◯ ∘	∘ ◯	◯ ∘ ∘	∘ ◯ ∘
garden	machine	motorbike	museum
also	July	photograph	suggestion
	across	ambulance	professor
	perhaps		

5 Monitor stress in these words.

> **Extension**
>
> If the students own dictionaries or there is a class set of dictionaries in which pronunciation and stress are marked, encourage them to make use of them. Set an exercise in which you give them ten or more new words (perhaps words that they are going to meet in the next few units of their coursebook) to look up in the dictionary. They have to find the word, note the stress pattern given and 'transfer' that to small and big circles over the word written in their notebooks.
>
> In some dictionaries a *secondary stress* is marked in some words either before or after the *main stress* (or primary stress). At this stage it is perhaps best to tell students to ignore any secondary stress marks that come after (i.e. to the right of) the main stress. These are, in any case, fairly uncommon. Much more common are words that have a secondary stress *before* the main stress. You may want to tell students that in some of these words, when they are used in a sentence, the main stress moves to the position of secondary stress. Examples of this are found in Unit 34.

Unit 31 Pronouncing unstressed syllables

> **Background**
>
> A distinction can be made between **strong** vowels and **weak** vowels. Strong vowels are those simple vowels (except /ə/ (as in <u>a</u>go)) and diphthongs listed in the *Key to phonetic symbols* on page viii. Stressed syllables always include a strong vowel. Weak vowels include /ə/ and the vowels in happ<u>y</u> and sit<u>u</u>ation which are sometimes represented by the symbols /i/ and /u/ respectively. Unstressed syllables may include a strong vowel or any of the weak vowels, although the weak vowel /ə/ is the most common vowel in unstressed syllables.

1 Tell students that the vowel /ə/ is very common in unstressed syllables in English (although it is not the *only* vowel found in unstressed syllables) and that it has the name 'schwa' (pronounced /ʃwɑː/). It is useful to give it a name to make it easy to refer to.

2 *Answers*

◯ ∘	∘ ◯ ∘	◯ ∘ ∘ ∘
1 answ<u>er</u>	2 import<u>a</u>nt	3 calc<u>u</u>lat<u>or</u>

⭕ ⚬ ⚬   ⚬ ⭕⚬ ⚬   ⚬ ⭕ ⚬   ⭕ ⚬
4 visit<u>or</u>   5 Australi<u>a</u>n or Austral<u>ia</u>n 6 dist<u>a</u>nt

⭕ ⚬   ⭕ ⚬   ⭕ ⚬
7 weath<u>er</u>   8 mirr<u>or</u>   9 wom<u>a</u>n

⚬ ⭕ ⚬   ⚬ ⭕⚬ ⚬   ⭕ ⚬
10 c<u>o</u>mput<u>er</u>   11 Americ<u>a</u>n   12 pregn<u>a</u>nt

If it is spoken slowly and carefully, 'Australian' is usually said with four syllables, otherwise it usually has three. Notice that the vowel in the second syllable of 'calculator' can be pronounced either /ə/ or /u/.

3 During repetition, monitor stress and the pronunciation of /ə/.

4 & 5 During repetition, pairwork and reporting back, monitor pronunciation of names of jobs. Check stress and the pronunciation of /ə/ in the final syllable.

> **Extension**
>
> Ask students to copy a sentence down from their coursebooks, and first try to predict which vowels will be pronounced /ə/ by underlining them. Then they listen to you saying the sentence or to a recording of it to check their predictions.

Unit 32 Rhythm

> **Background**
>
> A number of common words have two pronunciations, sometimes called their 'strong' and 'weak' forms. The strong forms are used when the words are given special emphasis or said on their own, and their weak forms are used on other occasions. These words are normally said with their weak forms and are important in giving English its characteristic rhythm. The weak forms of most of these words include the vowel sound /ə/.
>
> Words with weak forms that include /ə/ are: *a, am, an, and, are, as, at, but, can, could, do, does, for, from, had, has, have, her, must, of, shall, should, some, than, that, the, them, there, to, us, was, were, would*.
>
> Many learners tend to use the strong forms of these words where native speakers of English would use the weak forms, and for most students the tasks in this unit, which concentrates on the weak forms of just three of these words – 'of', 'to' and 'and' – will be useful. Other work on this topic can be found in Units 54 and 55 in Part 7.

2 *Answers*

1 A bottle <u>of</u> milk.
2 I'll go <u>and</u> see.
3 I've nothing <u>to</u> say.

4 A hundred <u>and</u> forty.
5 I'm going <u>to</u> London.
6 I have <u>to</u> go.

7 A piece <u>of</u> cake.

8 The first <u>of</u> October.

9 My mother <u>and</u> father.

10 I've lots <u>to</u> do.

11 A type <u>of</u> bread.

12 What's six <u>and</u> eight?

3 Rewind and repeat. Pause at the end of each sentence to give students time to repeat and check their answers.

During repetition, monitor the pronunciation of 'of', 'to' and 'and'.

4 *Answers*

fish and chips   bread and butter   cheese and biscuits

coffee and cake   apple pie and cream

5 Monitor pronunciation of 'and'.

6 This is a 'round-the-class' activity. Explain that each student has to try to outdo the previous one in the amount they are going to eat. Student A says: 'I'm really hungry. When I get home I'm going to have some bread and butter.' Student B then has to beat that by saying: 'I'm going to have bread and butter, and fish and chips.' Student C adds 'apple pie and cream', etc. Student E finishes with: 'I'm going to have bread and butter, fish and chips, apple pie and cream, biscuits and cheese, and coffee and cake.' Do this two or three times with different students. In a large class nominate students to speak.

Encourage students to try to speak fairly fluently without long hesitations. Monitor the pronunciation of 'and'.

7 Ask each student to think of another food combination. Encourage them to be imaginative (e.g. cornflakes and mustard, spaghetti and custard!). Then repeat the 'round-the-class' activity described in **6** using their own food combinations rather than 'bread and butter', etc. Stop each 'round' when there are five or six items on the menu. For the first few rounds write each new food combination on the board as it is added to help students remember. Then, if it doesn't interfere too much with fluency, play a few rounds in which students have to remember what other students have said up to that point and add a food combination themselves.

Again, monitor the pronunciations of 'and'.

Unit 33 More on rhythm

Background

By the term 'rhythm' we mean here the patterns of stressed syllables that are found in a sentence. Stressed syllables may follow one another as in

○ ○ ◯ ◯

It's a good book.   Or they may be separated by intervening unstressed syllables as in the examples in **1** in the Student's Book.

2 *Answers*

2 What did he say?	Five pounds an hour.	2
1 Shall we dance?	I'll call the police.	3
2 What do you earn?	He told me to rest.	3
2 Here is your change.	Thanks very much.	2
1 Where's it gone?	On the roof.	1
2 Give me your purse.	Yes, of course.	1

Monitor rhythm: that is, check that syllables are appropriately stressed or unstressed.

3 *Answers*

What did he say?	He told me to rest.
Shall we dance?	Yes, of course.
What do you earn?	Five pounds an hour.
Here is your change.	Thanks very much.
Where's it gone?	On the roof.
Give me your purse.	I'll call the police.

While the pairs say the conversations, monitor rhythm in the sentences.

> **Extension**
>
> While checking the answers, ask students questions about the conversations. For example, 'Who might be talking?' 'What are they talking about?' 'Where are they talking?' etc.

4 & 5 In these dialogues a fairly regular pattern of rhythm is established and repeated. In each dialogue the rhythm is slightly different with a different number of unstressed syllables between stressed words in each case. Monitor rhythm during performance of the conversation written by students.

> **Background**
>
> So far, the term 'stress' has been used to refer to the stressed syllable in individual words or stressed syllables in short phrases. When a word or phrase is used in a sentence, however, these syllables may or may not be stressed. The difference is sometimes referred to as 'word stress' and 'sentence stress' or 'prominence'. This is developed further in Part 6.

Unit 34 Rhythm and moving stress

> **Background**
>
> Many words have both a primary stressed syllable and a secondary stressed syllable earlier in the word. For example, ˌJapaˈnese. When these words are used in connected speech (that is, when the words are said in a context, not on their own) the main stress frequently moves away from

the primary to the secondary stressed syllable. For example:

   A 'Japanese 'businessman

This is often referred to as 'stress shift'. Stress shift happens particularly when the word is immediately followed by another stressed syllable. In the phrase *A Japanese translator* the stress is more likely to remain on the last syllable:

   A ˌJapa'nese trans'lator

Although stress shift can occur in any word with both primary and secondary stress, it is most often found in adjectives.

1 On the recording:

A: Do you want to see a photo of the English class I've been teaching?

B: Mmm. That's a good photo, isn't it? They look a very mixed group of students.

A: Yes, they are. They're all from different countries – all European and Asian, though.

B: So where are they all from?

A: Well, you've met Tomo, haven't you?

B: Yes, he was at the party, wasn't he?

A: Yes, that's right. He's a doctor. He's Japanese. Well, you can see him at the back on the right.

B: Yes, I recognise him.

A: And the other three students along the back are a journalist – she's Swedish. That's the one next to Tomo.

B: I see.

A: And then next to her is a dentist. She's Chinese.

B: They've got lots of different jobs, haven't they?

A: Amazing variety. At the back on the left is a diplomat. She's Spanish. Very important, too, I think.

B: Really?

A: Then next to her is a businessman. He's Taiwanese. Then at the front on the left is a teacher. He's Norwegian.

B: And then who are the two on the other side of Tomo?

A: Well, the woman next to Tomo is an actress. She's Italian. And then at the front next to her is a farmer. He's Portuguese.

Answers

Japanese – doctor	Taiwanese – businessman
Swedish – journalist	Norwegian – teacher
Chinese – dentist	Italian – actress
Spanish – diplomat	Portuguese – farmer

2 *Answers*

∘ ∘ ○	○ ∘	∘ ○	○ ∘	∘ ∘ ○
Japanese	Swedish	Chinese	Spanish	Taiwanese

∘ ○ ∘	∘ ○ ∘∘	∘ ∘ ○
Norwegian	Italian	Portuguese

3 Rewind and repeat. Pause after each word to give students time to repeat.

4 Explain that in some words in English, particularly longer words, there is sometimes a difference between stress when the word is said on its own and when it is said in a context. If this MOVING STRESS happens, stress always moves to an earlier syllable in the word. In the nationalities given here, for example, stress can move away from the last syllable to the first syllable in the word if another stressed syllable immediately follows the word.

Ask students to look at this in the example given in the Student's Book:

    o o O   O o o   O o

He's Japanese.   but   He's a Japanese doctor.

You can explain this by saying that the stress in 'doc-' pushes the stress in '-ese' away from it to an earlier syllable.

Answers

1 Japanese ✓	5 Taiwanese ✓
2 Swedish ✗	6 Norwegian ✗
3 Chinese ✓	7 Italian ✗
4 Spanish ✗	8 Portuguese ✓

5 Explain that for some numbers, too, stress when the number is said on its own can be different when the word is said in context, particularly when another stressed syllable immediately follows it.

6 Rewind and repeat. Pause after each word to give students time to repeat. During repetition, monitor moving stress.

7 Tell students to look at the pictures. Ask them questions like this:
Where does Emma live?
What number does Bob live at?
What's Ann's address?
Students answer as in the conversations in **5**. Correct when stress placement goes wrong. Students then work in pairs to make similar conversations.

Part 5 Sounds in connected speech

Aims and organisation

This section presents and practises differences between the pronunciation of words and phrases when they are said in isolation or at a slow speed (as they often are in the classroom), and when they are said in **connected speech**. In connected speech words generally flow together and are spoken at a speed that many learners consider very fast.

Unit 35
Slow speech and connected speech. Focus on understanding questions spoken at normal speed.

Unit 36
Common words and phrases in connected speech.

Unit 37
Linking words together: words that end with a consonant with words that begin with a vowel.

Unit 38
Linking words together: words that end with a vowel with words that begin with a consonant.

Unit 39
Linking words together: words that end with a consonant with words that begin with a consonant.

Unit 40
Sounds that link words: /w/ and /j/.

Unit 41
Sounds that link words: /r/.

Unit 42
Sounds that are missed out.

General notes

Before starting units in Part 5, it will be useful to explain to students that the features of pronunciation they are going to hear and practise are *not* features of very fast speech or of 'lazy' speech. They are found in the normal speech of a native speaker of Southern British English (and native speakers with many other accents, too) when, for example, they are having a conversation with another native speaker. By studying these aspects of pronunciation, students should find it easier to understand connected speech.

The emphasis in the section is on *listening* to the differences between the pronunciation of slow speech and connected speech, rather than on students producing these differences in their own speech. To sound like a native speaker of English a learner will have to incorporate these features of pronunciation into their speech, but if they don't, they should still be able to make themselves easily understood.

Notes on each unit

Unit 35 Slow speech and connected speech

In both Units 35 and 36 students are encouraged to make use of contextual clues to complete the tasks and, more generally, to help them make sense of connected speech.

2 On the recording (answers to **1** in bold):

1 A: Can you see my briefcase?   B: **It's over there.**
2 A: How many men were in the car?   B: **There were five of them.**
3 A: What time is it?   B: **Ten past seven.**
4 A: Can you help me open this bottle, please?   B: **Can't you do it?**
5 A: When will you arrive?   B: **As soon as I can.**
6 A: Excuse me, have you taken my coat by mistake?
   B: **I don't think so.**
7 A: Have you seen the film?   B: **Yeah, it's quite good.**
8 A: You don't look very well.   B: **I've got a cold.**
9 A: Well, are we going to the theatre?
   B: **I thought you said 'no'.**
10 A: When are you going to clean the car?
   B: **Perhaps I could do it tomorrow.**

3 *Answers*
a) 8   b) 2   c) 4   d) 1   e) 5   f) 6   g) 3   h) 7

4 Rewind and repeat. Pause at the end of each conversation to give students time to write down the question.

Answers
a) What do you do?
b) What have you got there?
c) Have you got a light?
d) Have you been here long?
e) Where are you going?
f) What's the matter?
g) Do you know him?
h) What time is it?

5 & 6 In repetition and pairwork, encourage students to say the conversations at normal speed. Monitor and correct if necessary.

> **Extension**
>
> As a further awareness activity for students, play a very short extract from any recordings you have of English spoken at 'conversational' speed by native speakers. Students should try to write down what is being said. Play the recording as many times as is necessary. If appropriate, ask students to consider how this conversational English differs from the slow, careful English they are perhaps used to hearing in the classroom.

Unit 36 Common words and phrases in connected speech

1 Students could work in pairs or alone to think about possible answers. Ask for suggestions for all the sentences before listening to the recording.

Answers
1 or   2 an   3 and   4 or   5 are   6 of   7 Are
8 of   9 a   10 have

2 Rewind and repeat. Monitor the pronunciation of 'or', 'an', 'and', 'are', 'of', 'a' and 'have'. Correct if they are not pronounced with the sound /ə/ ('schwa').

It is important not to emphasise these words or emphasise the sound /ə/ when you try to show, during correction, how they should be pronounced. The words should be said quickly and with their 'weak' not 'strong' forms (that is, /ə/ not /ɔː/, etc. – see notes to Unit 32 for more information on this). One simple way to avoid giving them emphasis is to be sure to say them in the contexts given here rather than isolating the words and saying them on their own.

3 Before a word that begins with a consonant sound, 'are', 'of' and 'or' are usually pronounced /ə/. Before a word that begins with a vowel sound, they are usually pronounced /ər/, /əv/ and /ər/.

4 The missing parts are all common phrases used in conversations.

Answers
1 A: **Excuse me.**   B: Yes, what can I do for you?
2 A: What is it?   B: **I don't know.**
3 A: What time is it?   B: (It's) **About eight** (o'clock).
4 A: **Thank you.**   B: **That's all right.**
5 A: **Are you going to go?**   B: Yes.

5 *Answers*
1 …want to…   4 …going to get you…going to meet you…
2 …got to…   5 You've got to teach them about…
3 Because…

Extension

Look at the words of current pop songs that your students are familiar with for other examples of how connected speech is shown in written English.

Unit 37 Linking words together: Consonant + Vowel

When explaining the purpose of this unit, point out that the links are between a consonant *sound* at the end of words with a following vowel *sound*. Some words end with a vowel *letter* but with a consonant *sound* and some students may find this confusing. Explain this with a few examples. Write the words 'one', 'these' and 'quite' on the board. Ask whether the final letter of each is a vowel or consonant. Then ask whether the final sound in each is a vowel or consonant.

1 Encourage students to speak at normal speed with no gap between the words marked. Monitor the links between the words.

2 In this activity, the student's partner monitors and corrects where necessary.

3 *Suggested answers*
   1 a crowd of people   2 a map of the world   3 a box of matches   4 a bunch of flowers   5 a block of flats
   6 a couple of hours   7 a piece of cake   8 a chest of drawers

4 In monitoring, check (a) that 'of' is pronounced /ə/ (or /əv/), and (b) that consonant and vowel are being linked together.

5 *Suggested answers*
   1 You put up an umbrella.
   2 You put out a light.
   3 You put on your clothes.
   4 You take off your clothes.
   5 You take up golf (or any sport or hobby).
   6 You turn off the radio; a light; the cooker.
   7 You turn up the radio; the cooker.
   8 You get on a bus.
   9 You get in a car.
   10 You keep off the grass.

6 Monitor the links between consonant and vowel.

Unit 38 Linking words together: Vowel + Consonant

As with Unit 37, when explaining the purpose of this unit, point out that the links are between vowel *sounds* at the ends of words with following consonant *sounds*. In task 1 many of the words ending in vowel *sounds* end in the consonant letters 'y', 'w' or 'r'.

1 & 2 Monitor the links between vowel and following consonant marked in **1**.

3 The words in the left-hand column end with a consonant sound. The words in the right-hand column start with a vowel sound.

Suggested answers

post‿office, customs‿officer, headache, smoke‿alarm, travel‿agent,

shop‿assistant, North‿Africa, musical‿instrument

Monitor the links between consonant and vowel sounds shown in the answers above.

4 The words in the left-hand column end with a vowel sound. The words in the right-hand column start with a consonant sound.

Suggested answers

sore‿throat, power‿station, Sahara‿Desert, flower‿shop,

company‿director, computer‿keyboard, motorbike, letterbox

Monitor the links between vowel and consonant sounds shown in the answers above.

5 Give pairs time to think of connections and then ask them to report their answers to the class. Monitor links between consonant and vowel sounds and between vowel and consonant sounds in the phrases.

> **Extension**
>
> For homework ask students to collect more 'compound words' like the ones in **3** and **4**, perhaps from their coursebooks. They should decide if the link is between consonant + vowel, vowel + consonant, consonant + consonant, or vowel + vowel. Have students report their compound words to the class. Monitor the links. Collect the examples together and use them at a later date in a task similar to that in **3** to **5**.

Unit 39 Linking words together: Consonant + Consonant

> **Background**
>
> This unit looks at some common changes that take place in the pronunciation of certain word-final consonants in connected speech. The focus is on the changes to the pronunciation of the sounds /t/, /d/ and /n/ when they are followed by words that begin with the sounds /m/, /b/ and /p/. The process of changing the pronunciation of sounds such as /t/, /d/ and /n/ to make them sound more like the following sound is often referred to as 'assimilation'. For example, in the phrase *brown bag* the /n/ sound at the end of *brown* is said almost as /m/ as the tongue and lips move quickly into position to produce the /b/ sound at the beginning of *bag*.

Notice that this book does not look at the details of these changes in pronunciation. Although it is perhaps not of great importance for students to make such changes in their own speech, it is useful for them to be aware that such changes take place to help them understand the connected speech of native speakers. For more information on the details of these changes, see Wells (1990) or Gimson (1989, Ch. 11) in the list of *Recommended books* on page 3.

1 *Answers*

1 might	2 clean	3 felt	4 rained	5 want
6 need	7 thin	8 third	9 begin	

3 Rewind and repeat. Pause at the end of each item to give students time to repeat. Monitor sound changes at the end of the words when they are said in the sentences. Encourage students to run the consonants together and pronounce the consonant sounds in their 'connected speech' form.

4 & 5 Monitor pronunciation at the end of the first word in each phrase.

Unit 40 Sounds that link words: /w/ and /j/ ('y')

Background

When a word that ends in a vowel is followed by a word that begins with a vowel, speakers will often insert a very short /w/ or /j/ ('y') sound to link the vowels together to make the flow of speech more smooth and to avoid a 'gap' between the words. The choice of either /w/ or /j/ depends on the vowel that ends the first word. If the vowel is produced with the highest part of the tongue close to the *front* of the mouth (/iː/, /eɪ/, /aɪ/, /ɔɪ/) then the linking sound will be /j/. If the vowel is produced with the highest part of the tongue close to the *back* of the mouth (/uː/, /aʊ/, /əʊ/) then the linking sound will be /w/.

1 Conversation on the recording:

ALAN: Do you know it's Phil's birthday on Thursday?

SUE: I'd forgotten all about it.

ALAN: I suppose we should buy him a present.

SUE: And we really ought to have a party for him.

ALAN: Well, what can we get him?

SUE: It depends how much we want to pay.

ALAN: If we pay about £10 we could get him something really nice.

SUE: What about a new umbrella? He's got that old blue one, but it's all broken. He should throw it away.

ALAN: That's a great idea. And it won't be too expensive. And what about a party?

SUE: Well, we could invite a few friends around here. How about Thursday evening?

ALAN: We could, but I know he's got an interview on Friday, and he might want to get ready for that.

SUE: Well, let's wait till the weekend. Anyway, more people will be free on Saturday.

ALAN: OK. I'll buy the present, and you arrange the party.

SUE: Fine.

Answers

1 On Thursday.   2 An umbrella.   3 On Saturday.

3 Monitor the /w/ link between the vowels marked.

4 Monitor the /j/ link between the vowels marked.

5 *Answers*

1 Who‿are you?

2 Germany‿imports gold.

3 Don't argue‿about it.

4 Coffee‿or tea?

5 I've been to‿Amsterdam.

6 Tomorrow‿afternoon.

7 Go‿away!

8 Hello,‿Ann!

9 Goodbye,‿Ann.

10 They weigh‿about five kilos.

6 Monitor the /w/ and /j/ links between the vowels.

> **Extension**
>
> You could ask better students to try to discover when /w/ is used to link the words and when /j/. If necessary, give a clue by telling them to pay attention to the vowel sound that comes before the linking sound.

Unit 41 Sounds that link words: /r/

> **Background**
>
> In Southern British English, words said on their own never end in the sound /r/. However, when words that end in the *letters* 'r' or 're' are followed by a word beginning with a vowel then a /r/ sound is inserted. This is often referred to as the 'linking-r'. This typically happens when the word said on its own ends in one of the vowels /ɑː/, /ɔː/, /ɜː/, /ə/, /ɪə/, /eə/ or /ʊə/. This linking-r is very common and is practised here.
>
> Less common, and even disapproved of by some people, is a /r/ sound inserted when the word ends in one of these vowels but not with the *letter* 'r'. This is often referred to as the 'intrusive /–r/'. For example, in the phrase '*America and China*' some speakers will insert a /r/ sound between *America* and *and*. This is not practised here, although you may think it useful to make students aware of it.

1 Monitor the /r/ link between the vowels.

3 *Answers*
1 Is the **door** open?
2 They've forgotten **their** air tickets.
3 She's my **mother**-in-law.
4 He started his new job a **year** ago.
5 I've been waiting for an **hour** and a half.
6 My **brother** is older than me.
7 Do you live **far** away?
8 **Neither** am I.

Monitor the /r/ links between vowels.

4 *Suggested answers*
October/November   mother/father   under/over
summer/winter   before/after   near/far   brother/sister
here/there   sooner/later   car/helicopter   beer/water

5 Monitor /r/ links between the first word and the word 'and'.

Unit 42 Short sounds and sounds that are missed out

Background
When words begin with the sound /h/, this sound is often made very short or may be lost altogether in connected speech.

Some very common words have a strong and weak form (for more information see the notes to Unit 32). These include *had, has, have, he, her, him, his* and *who*, which are pronounced with an initial /h/ sound in their strong forms. This sound may be missed out in their weak forms.

It is not necessary for students to incorporate these features into their own speech for them to be understood. It is, however, useful for students to be aware of these features of the pronunciation of native speakers to help them understand. This is why the emphasis in this unit is on understanding and identification alone.

2 *Answers*
1 across   2 agree   3 arrive   4 awake   5 abroad
6 afraid   7 alone   8 about away

4 *Answers*
1 A: Is that ̶him over there?
  B: Who?
  A: The man w̶h̶o took your handbag?
2 A: He wasn't at home.
  B: No, I think ̶he's on holiday.
3 A: How's Tom these days?
  B: Didn't you hear about ̶his heart attack?

4 A: It says <u>h</u>ere, the Queen's coming.

　B: Where?

　A: <u>H</u>ere.

　B: I do <u>h</u>ope we'll be able to see ~~h~~er.

5 A: What are you children fighting about?

　B: It's MY book.

　A: <u>H</u>IS book's over there.

　B: <u>H</u>ER book's over there. This one's mine!

5 *Answers*

him, who, he('s), his, her

'h' *is* pronounced when these words are at the start of a sentence.

6 Monitor the pronunciation of the 'h' letters underlined.

Extension

If you have worked through all of the units in Part 5, it may be useful to give students the opportunity to see how all the features they have studied are found in connected speech. To do this, begin by reminding students of the features they have looked at. For example, write the summary below on a handout or on the board:

Common features of connected speech are:

1　Links between consonants and vowels　　　e.g. Seven oranges.

2　Links between vowels and consonants　　　e.g. Two books.

3　Links between the consonants /t/, /d/ and /n/

　　and the consonants /m/, /b/ and /p/　　　　e.g. It's that man.

　　　　　　　　　　　　　　　　　　　　　　e.g. A good party.

　　　　　　　　　　　　　　　　　　　　　　e.g. Better than
　　　　　　　　　　　　　　　　　　　　　　　　　before.

4　Sounds that link words: /w/　　　　　　　e.g. How often?

　　　　　　　　　　　　/j/ ('y')　　　　　　e.g. Three apples.

　　　　　　　　　　　　/r/　　　　　　　　e.g. Car engine.

5　Sounds that are very short　　　　　　　　e.g. South America.

6　Sounds that are missed out: for example /h/　e.g. Can you see him?

Then ask students to work in pairs and predict features of connected speech that might be found in given sentences. You could give sentences from dialogues in their coursebooks, or you could give some of the following questions. Features likely to be found in connected speech are marked.

1　Is ~~h~~e still in bed?

2　Anything else?

3　Can you open it?

4　How often?

5　Can I help you?

6　Have you got my ticket?

7　Is it far away?

8　When are you off?

9　Do you like it?

10　Will you be in?

11　What did you buy ~~h~~im?

12　Was it a good party?

Part 6 Intonation

Aims and organisation

In Part 6 students practise features of the **intonation** of English. Attention is focused on **prominent** words (that is, words that stand out from surrounding words) and **non-prominent words, tones** (falls and rises in the pitch of the voice), and **tonic words** (the words where the pitch movement starts).

Unit 43
Listening for prominent and non-prominent words; practice of prominent and non-prominent words.

Unit 44
More practice of prominent and non-prominent words; focus on non-prominent repeated words.

Unit 45
More practice of prominent and non-prominent words; focus on non-prominent grammar words.

Unit 46
Listening for falling and rising tones.

Unit 47
Understanding the reasons for using a falling or a rising tone; more practice of tones.

Unit 48
Practice of a second rising tone: the falling-rising tone.

Unit 49
Listening for tonic words; more practice of tones.

Unit 50
Understanding the reasons for the choice of tonic word.

General notes

Background
In the approach to intonation used here, three things are important: whether a word is made **prominent** or not; what kind of pitch

movement (**tone**) is used; and on which word (the **tonic word**) this pitch movement begins. These will be explained in a little more detail below: prominent words in the notes for Unit 43, tone in Unit 46, and tonic words in Unit 49. Note that it is not *necessary* to read this background information before teaching any of the units in Part 6, although you may find it helps, particularly in answering any questions your students have about intonation. Nor is it necessary to explain any of the detail to students, although for better students you may find it useful to do so.

The notes in Part 6 give only a very brief description of the approach to intonation used here. If you want further information, look at either Brazil (1985) or Bradford (1988), details of which can be found in the list of *Recommended books* on page 3.

Notes on each unit

Unit 43 Prominent words

Background

Prominent words

Prominent words stand out from the surrounding words. This may be because they are said slightly louder than others, at a slightly higher pitch, or are said with a falling or rising pitch. For example, if you listen to sentence 5, task 1 in Unit 43 in the Student's Book, you should hear the word 'sure' as prominent in 'I'm <u>sure</u> she will'.

Although we talk here only about prominent and non-prominent words, if you listen to sentence 6, task 1, Unit 43, you will hear that it is only the first syllable in 'lovely' in 'It's a <u>love</u>ly place' that is prominent. It is a useful simplification to say that the *word* '<u>love</u>ly' is prominent, even though only one of its syllables is prominent. Any word that has at least one prominent syllable will be said to be prominent. (In some of the tasks in Part 6 prominent words are shown in capital letters. The *whole* word is written in capital letters even though, in words with more than one syllable, only one of the syllables is actually prominent.)

It is important to distinguish here between what we mean by 'stress' and what we mean by 'prominence'. When you look up in a dictionary a word with more than one syllable, one of these syllables is marked as having stress; for example, *com 'pu ter*. Some words will have two stresses, one primary and the other secondary; for example, *ˌJa paˈnese*. When a word is used in speech, it may or may not be given prominence. If it is, then the prominent syllable in the word will be the one that the dictionary indicates is stressed.

For example, a dictionary will say that the word 'raining' has stress on the first syllable, and that the word 'again' has stress on the second. If you listen to sentence 8, task 1, Unit 43, you will hear that 'raining' is prominent, but 'again' is not. So not all stressed syllables are prominent, but if a word *is* made prominent, then the stressed syllable becomes the prominent one. In words with both primary and secondary stress, the primary stressed one will normally be made prominent, but sometimes it may be the one having secondary stress.

A word will be made prominent if it is chosen from a range of words that are possible in a context. So, for example, in sentence 9, task 1, Unit 43 'He's a postman', the word 'postman' is made prominent, but not 'he'. This is because 'postman' is a choice from a range of jobs (teacher, manager, librarian, etc.). However, if the topic of conversation is a particular male person, then the speaker must use 'he' – there is no other choice. Many learners of English tend to make more words prominent than they need to, and Units 44 and 45 give practice by focusing on words that are rarely prominent – repeated words and certain grammar words, particularly pronouns. These are normally non-prominent, because they are rarely a selection from a range of possible words.

1 *Answers*

1 (Thank) you.

2 I'm (tired).

3 (Chris) did.

4 It's getting (late).

5 I'm (sure) she will.

6 It's a (lovely) place.

7 She's in the (sitting) room.

8 It's (raining) again.

9 He's a (postman).

10 We had a (great) time.

2 Rewind and repeat. Pause at the end of each sentence to give students time to repeat. During repetition, monitor placement of prominence in sentences.

Extension

Follow a similar procedure using short recorded sentences from the students' coursebook.

3 *Answers*

a) 3   b) 1   c) 10   d) 8   e) 6   f) 9   g) 2

h) 4   i) 7   j) 5

4 For example, students say:

A: Who cooked dinner?
B: Chris did.

Monitor placement of prominence in the sentences.

Giving more details

5 *Suggested answers*

chicken pie/salad/omelette/soup; tomato salad/omelette/soup; cheese salad/omelette; cherry pie; apple pie

6 Monitor prominence. Both words are to be made prominent.

7 & 8 Monitor prominence. When the word is repeated, it should not be made prominent.

Unit 44 Repeated words and prominence

1 Notice that the repeated word is not made prominent. Monitor prominence. Check that the repeated word in each is not made prominent.

On the recording:

3 A: Have you got any in   B: NO, only LIGHT blue, I'm AFRAID.
   dark blue?

4 A: Are you feeling better? B: Oh, YES. MUCH better.

5 A: Shall we meet at one?   B: CAN we make it HALF PAST one?

6 A: And the winning   B: That's MY number.
   number is 5-4-9.

7 A: He's an artist, isn't he? B: YES, a VERY GOOD artist,
                                 ACTUALLY.

8 A: Did you say Tom was   B: NO, the BACK garden.
   in the front garden?

2 In this activity, monitoring is to be done by one of the students in each group. If organising students into groups of three is difficult, this should be done in pairs with the teacher monitoring.

3 *Answer* b

4 *Answers*

In the middle	is a <u>big</u> circle.
Above it	is a <u>small</u> circle.

On the left of the big circle	is a <u>small</u> <u>triangle</u>.
On the right	is a <u>big</u> triangle.

Point out that the repeated words are not made prominent.

5 Demonstrate this first with a better student. Draw a picture on a piece of paper and describe it to the student who should try to draw it on the board. Then compare your picture with what the student drew and point out any differences. During pairwork, monitor prominence particularly on 'big', 'small', 'circle', 'square' and 'triangle'. Draw attention to repetitions where it is inappropriate to make the word prominent.

> **Extension**
>
> If possible, record one or two pairs doing the task and note any difficulties with prominence. Replay the recording to the class and point out the problems. Ask what *should* have been said.

Unit 45 More on prominent and non-prominent words

1–3 The point of the task, and the explanation that should be elicited or given in **2**, is that it is not only repeated items that are often non-prominent, but also *pronouns*, which are effectively another way of 'repeating' a noun.

1 *Answers*
1 them   2 him   3 her   4 there   5 he   6 one
7 there   8 us

3 Monitor prominence. Check that the pronouns written in **1** are not prominent.

4 *Most likely answers*
1 packet   2 bunch   3 jar   4 loaf   5 tin   6 bottle
7 jar   8 packet/box   9 bunch   10 carton

6 Rewind and repeat. Pause at the end of each line to give students time to repeat. Read through the notes given about certain words in the conversation. Explain further if necessary.

7 During pairwork, monitor prominent and non-prominent words.

Unit 46 Falling and rising tones

Background

Tone

There are two major tones in English – a falling tone and a rising tone. When a speaker chooses a falling tone, they are indicating that what is said is seen as 'news' for the hearer. When a rising tone is chosen, they are indicating that what is said is seen as something the hearer already knows. It is best to explain this with examples. We can take these from task 1, Unit 47.

We might expect the following tones in B's reply in:

A: When are you going to New York?

B: I'm flying at ten o'clock.

The reason for the first tone is that B assumes A's question, 'When are you going...?' to mean 'When are you flying...?' (if the conversation takes place outside the USA, then flying is the most likely way to get to New York, so this is a reasonable assumption). 'I'm flying...' is therefore assumed to be known by A. '...at ten o'clock' is, however, clearly 'news' to A.

We might expect the following tones in B's reply in:

A: Do I turn it on with this switch?

B: Press the red one, not the black one.

In this case, A and B can presumably see that the switch A is indicating is black. It is not necessary, then, for B to present this fact as 'news' to A. It is, however, necessary for B to tell A what switch *should* be pressed, and so we have a falling tone on 'Press the red one'.

Two forms of both the rising and falling tone are used in English. The rising tone may be either a simple rise (↗) or a fall followed by a rise (∨↗). In Part 6 no distinction in meaning is made between them, which at this level is a reasonable simplification. There *is* a difference, however. Although both present what is said as something already known to the hearer, the simple rise is generally only used by a speaker who is 'in control' of speaking. In some situations it is very clear who is in control – a teacher in a classroom or a doctor talking to a patient. In others, a speaker is in control because there is no obvious hearer – a newsreader on radio or TV, for example. And within conversations, a speaker may take control to try to prevent herself or himself being interrupted – when telling a joke or story, for example. In such circumstances, it is only usually the 'controlling' speaker who uses the simple rising tone.

2 *Answers*

1 a) I went to London … (↘)   b) … on Saturday. (↗)
2 a) David … (↗)   b) … works in a bookshop. (↘)
3 a) There's some cake … (↘)   b) … in the kitchen. (↗)
4 a) In Hong Kong … (↘)   b) … last year. (↘)
5 a) I'm fairly sure … (↗)   b) … it's upstairs. (↘)
6 a) Yes, … (↘)   b) … of course. (↘)
7 a) Turn left here … (↗)   b) … then go straight on. (↘)
8 a) Oh dear, … (↘)   b) … I *am* sorry. (↘)
9 a) I like it … (↗)   b) … very much. (↘)
10 a) I don't smoke … (↘)   b) … thank you. (↘)

3 Rewind and repeat. Pause at the end of each sentence half to give students time to repeat. During repetition, monitor tone in the sentence halves.

4 Monitor the tones in the complete sentences.

5 *Answers*

a) 2   b) 3   c) 1   d) 9   e) 5   f) 10   g) 7   h) 6
i) 4   j) 8

6 For example, students say:

A: What does your son do now?

B: David works in a bookshop.

Monitor tone in the second part of each conversation.

7 You may want to point out that in these examples and in the examples in **9**, the two people are talking about the same subject even though the words they use to describe it are different. So, for example, 'seeing a film' is the same as 'going to the cinema', and 'going to a restaurant' is the same as 'going out to eat'.

8 Rewind and repeat. Pause at the end of each sentence to give students time to repeat. During repetition, monitor tones.

9 Monitor tones. Check that the same patterns of falling and rising tones are used as shown in **7**.

Unit 47 Reasons for falling and rising

1 & 2 *Answers*
   3 I'm flying (↗) at ten o'clock (↘).
   4 I've known him (↗) for years (↘).
   5 I've been learning French (↗) for six years (↘).
   6 Tuesday (↘) was the last time I saw him (↗).
   7 Press the red one (↘), not the black one (↗).
   8 Your papers (↗) are on the table (↘) in the kitchen (↘).

During pairwork monitor tones.

4 Falling tones are used in 'red' and 'blue' as they are information being given. A rising tone is used for 'my favourite' as the idea of favourites is already being talked about.
   During pairwork monitor tones.

Unit 48 A second rising tone

1 *Answers*
   1 b   2 a   3 c   4 a   5 b   6 b   7 a   8 b
   9 c   10 a

2 *Answers*
   1 S   2 D   3 D   4 D   5 D   6 S   7 S   8 D

3 Rewind and repeat. Pause at the end of each of B's sentences to give students time to write their answers.

Answers
   1 B: YES ↘ – I'd LOVE to. ↘
   2 B: NO ↘ – NOT YET. ↗
   3 B: YES ↘ – I THINK so. ↘↗
   4 B: NO ↘ – not REALLY. ↘↗
   5 B: BYE ↘↗ – see you TOMORROW. ↗
   6 B: PERHAPS ↘↗ – I don't KNOW yet. ↘↗
   7 B: REALLY ↘↗ – I THOUGHT they would. ↘↗
   8 B: on SUNDAY ↘ – IF the WEATHER'S good. ↘↗

4 Monitoring in this task is done by the student's partner. Help or adjudicate where necessary.

5 On the recording:
Portugal, Albufeira, Spain, Cadiz, France, Nice, Italy, Bari,
Morocco, Casablanca, Algeria, Oran, Tunisia, Sousse

7 Pause at the end of each line to give students time to repeat. During
repetition monitor tones.

8 & 9 Monitor tones during repetition and pairwork. It is not necessary
to insist on a falling-rising tone in the sections marked: a rising tone
could also be used.

Unit 49 Tonic words

Background

Tonic words

The word on which a falling or rising tone starts is here called the **tonic
word**. The following sentences are taken from Unit 49, task 2. In each the
tonic word is underlined.

It's on <u>top</u> of the bookcase.

With <u>milk</u>, please.

At five past <u>one</u>.

The choice of tonic word is important. Compare, for example, 'It's on top
of the <u>bookcase</u>', which might be said in answer to 'Where's the
newspaper?', and 'It's on <u>top</u> of the bookcase', which might be said in
response to 'I thought I put the newspaper on the bookcase.'

All tonic words are heard as prominent, but not all prominent words
are necessarily tonic words. In Unit 49, task 2(d) both 'five' and 'past' are
prominent, but only on 'past' is there a pitch movement. That is, only
'past' is a tonic word.

2 & 3 *Answers*

a) It's on (top) of the bookcase.   d) At five (past) one.

b) With (milk), please.   e) It's on top of the (bookcase).

c) At (five) past one.   f) (With) milk, please.

3 Rewind and repeat. Pause at the end of each sentence to give
students time to repeat and check their answers. During repetition,
monitor tonic words.

4 Students have to match the sentences in **2** with the contexts created
by the sentences in **4**. Consideration of placement of the tonic word
is important in doing this correctly.

4 & 5 *Answers*

1 f   2 c   3 e   4 b   5 a   6 d

6 & 7 *Answers*

1 A: Can I HELP you?
  B: I'm looking for a DRESS.
  A: They're on the SECOND floor.
  B: THANK you.

2 A: What do you THINK?
  B: I don't like the COLOUR.
  A: I thought you LIKED red.
  B: I prefer BLUE.

3 A: Shall we eat HERE?
  B: Let's sit over THERE.
  A: Under THAT tree?
  B: The OTHER one.

8 Rewind and repeat. Pause at the end of each sentence to give students time to repeat. During repetition, monitor placement of tonic words.

> **Extension**
>
> Many coursebooks and other supplementary materials include recordings of short two- or four-line conversations like these. Identify tonic words yourself in such conversations and then use them to do a task similar to that in **6** to **8**.

Unit 50 Predicting tones

1 & 2 *Answers*

1 A: Was it EXPENSIVE?
  B: QUITE expensive.
  A: How MUCH?
  B: A thousand POUNDS.

2 A: Is it still RAINING?
  B: I THINK so.
  A: HEAVILY?
  B: Not VERY.

3 A: What's on TV tonight?
  B: A HORROR film.
  A: Is it GOOD?
  B: I've HEARD it is.

3 Rewind and repeat. Pause at the end of each sentence to give students time to repeat. During repetition, monitor tones.

4 Many contexts are possible for each of these sentences. Notice that the falling tone in 4 is likely to indicate a definite acceptance, perhaps of an invitation. The falling-rising tone is likely to indicate some sort of reservation: 'I'd like to … but (I'm doing something else)'. During performance check (a) that the sentences are being said with the intonation shown, and (b) that the intonation is appropriate in the context that has been created.

Part 7 Sounds and grammar

Aims and organisation

In Part 7 attention is drawn to the relationship between grammar and pronunciation in certain common (and often problematic) areas. These are: the **'long'** and **'short'** (or contracted) forms of certain modal/ auxiliary verbs; the **weak** and **strong** forms of modal/auxiliary verbs, conjunctions and prepositions; the varying pronunciations of **'-ed' endings** in regular past participles; and the varying pronunciations of **'-s' endings** in third person present simple verbs and in plurals.

Unit 51
The weak and strong forms of *do, does* and *can*; the short (*don't, doesn't* and *can't*) and long forms of the negatives of these verbs.

Unit 52
The long and short forms of *would, should, had, will, shall, is, are, has, have* and *am*.

Unit 53
More practice of the long and short forms of *would, should, had, will, shall, is, are, has, have* and *am*.

Unit 54
The weak and strong forms of the conjunctions *and, or, but, as* and *than*.

Unit 55
The weak and strong forms of the prepositions *at, for, from, of* and *to*.

Unit 56
The pronunciation of the *'-ed'* ending of past simple tense verbs.

Unit 57
More practice of the *'-ed'* ending of past simple tense verbs.

Unit 58
The pronunciation of *'-s'* endings in plurals and third person simple present tense verbs (e.g. looks, runs).

Notes on each unit

Unit 51 Weak and strong forms; short and long forms

This unit is intended to introduce the idea of weak and strong forms, and short and long forms. For information on weak and strong forms, see the notes for Unit 32.

1 & 2 The weak forms of the verbs are shown in small letters.

1 Rewind and repeat for the last part of this task. Pause at the end of each sentence to give students time to repeat.

3 *Answers*

1 Do you like it?	Yes, very much.
2 Can we go now?	A bit later.
3 Does he live here?	No, next door.
4 Can I take two?	Yes, of course.
5 Does it hurt?	Not really.
6 When do you go back?	Tomorrow.
7 Why does she want to leave?	She's tired.
8 Where can we see one?	In a zoo.
9 How do you feel now?	Much better.

5 & 6 It may be useful to demonstrate these first. Write the questions on the board and ask a student the questions. He or she should answer with the short forms and you should place a tick or cross on the board as appropriate. When you have gathered the answers, report back the negative answers as in **6**.

During pairwork and reporting back, monitor the short forms.

> **Extension**
>
> Further work on weak and strong forms can be found in Units 32, 54 and 55.

Unit 52 Long and short forms of verbs

> **Background**
>
> These short forms are often referred to as 'contractions' or 'contracted forms'. Most short forms are verbs, although 'us' is also contracted to 's in, for example, 'Let's go'.

1 Use the tables for reference and to explain the difference between short and long forms and to point out that many very common verbs in English have short forms.

2 Play the conversation through once and ask the students just to listen. Then play it again, stopping at the end of each sentence to give students time to write their answers.

Answers

A: I'd like some of those apples, please. How much are they?

B: They're twelve pence each. How many would you like?

A: I'll have five, please.

B: There you are. Shall I put them in a bag for you?

A: Oh, would you? That's very kind of you.

B: Anything else?

A: No, that's all thanks. How much is that?

B: That'll be 60 pence, please.

A: Here's a £5 note.

B: Have you got anything smaller?

A: Er … oh, yes. I've got a pound coin.

3 Rewind and repeat. Pause at the end of each sentence to give students time to repeat. During repetition and pairwork make sure that students use the short forms where necessary in the dialogue.

4 A possible completion is:
The LONG form of these verbs is used in … questions.

> **Extension**
>
> Another place where the long form of the verbs is used, although this is not explicitly taught here, is when they occur at the end of a sentence. Compare
> 'Ann**'s** got it' with:
> 'Has Ann got it?'   'Yes, she **has**.'
> You could point this out to students.

6 & 7 These tasks practise the short forms of 'is' and 'have', and short forms with 'not'. Monitor these short forms in the descriptions in **5** and during pairwork in **6** and **7**.

Unit 53 More on the long and short forms of verbs

> **Background**
>
> In Unit 52 a simple rule was given about when the long forms of the words *would, should, had, will, shall, is, are, has, have* and *am* are used rather than their short forms: long forms tend to be used in questions, but short forms elsewhere. However, in fairly fast speech it is quite common for these words to take their short form if they follow 'wh-' questions words (what, who, when, where, how, etc.). Questions with 'wh-' words followed by short forms are practised in task 3 in Unit 53.
>
> Notice also that after certain sounds (/s/, /z/, /ʃ/, /tʃ/ and /dʒ/) the short form of 'is' is not used. So in 'How much is …?' 'is' takes its full form. You may want to point this out to students or to have the information to hand if students ask about the long form after 'How much…?'

1 *Answers*

How old are you?   I'm twenty-one.
Is she here?   No, she's in town.
When will you go?   I'll go tomorrow.
Shall we eat now?   I'd rather wait until later.
Have you been before? Yes, I've been twice.

2 Monitor long and short forms.

3 *Answers*

What's your name?   It's Rachel Jones.
When're they going?   They've got to be home by 11.
What's Jim got?   It's a present.
Where've you been?   I'm sorry. The train was late.
What're you doing?   I'm making dinner.

During repetition and pairwork, monitor short forms.

4 On the recording:
Mrs Jones: ... They're called Tom and Paul. Tom's five and Paul's seven. Tom's wearing football shorts and Paul's got jeans on, I think. They're both wearing T-shirts, and I think Tom's got a jacket with him. Tom's got fair hair and Paul's got dark hair – oh, but he's probably wearing a hat. And they've got their dog with them. And ... oh, thank goodness ... they've just walked through the door ...

Answers
Picture (b) is Tom and picture (d) is Paul.

5 Encourage students to produce short forms of the verbs. Monitor these.

6 Monitor use of short forms during pairwork.

Unit 54 Weak and strong forms of some conjunctions

1 *Answers*

1 a) Milk <u>but</u> no sugar.
   b) Milk <u>and</u> no sugar.
2 a) Paul <u>and</u> Alison.
   b) Paul <u>or</u> Alison.
3 a) It was small <u>but</u> very heavy.
   b) It was small <u>and</u> very heavy.
4 a) Jean <u>and</u> her friend.
   b) Jean <u>or</u> her friend.
5 a) <u>But</u> I want to go.
   b) <u>And</u> I want to go.
6 a) Red <u>or</u> green.
   b) Red <u>and</u> green.

2 Rewind and repeat. Pause at the end of each sentence to give students time to repeat. During repetition monitor the weak forms of these words.

3 Demonstrate this first with a better student. During pairwork monitor weak forms of 'and', 'or' and 'but'.

4 On the recording:
1 In January, London is colder than Athens. (T)
2 In July, Paris is about as wet as London. (T)
3 In July, Stockholm is sunnier than Athens. (F)
4 In January, Moscow is as sunny as Stockholm. (T)
5 In July, Athens is hotter than Moscow. (T)
6 In January, Paris is about the same temperature as Stockholm. (F)
7 In January, Stockholm is colder than London. (T)
8 In July, London is sunnier than Paris. (F)

5 Demonstrate this first with a better student. During pairwork monitor weak forms of 'as' and 'than'.

> **Extension**
>
> You could do a similar task using information the students have gathered about each other comparing such features as height, weight, age, etc.

Unit 55 Weak and strong forms of some prepositions

1 & 2 *Answers* (answers to **2** underlined):
1 He was looking .... the children in the park. [for/at]
2 I was at home .... six o'clock. [at/from]
3 They drove .... Glasgow last night. [from/to]
4 He had a drawing .... Rome. [of/from]
5 She picked up the ball and threw it ....
 her brother. [at/to]
6 Do you like this picture? It's a present ....Sue. [for/from]
7 The people .... France drink a lot of wine. [of/from]
8 She pointed .... the ship. [to/at]

3 Monitor the strong and weak forms of the prepositions.

4 Monitor the pronunciation of the prepositions given in the box in **1**.

5 *Answers*
1 S 2 W 3 W 4 S 5 S 6 W 7 S 8 S
9 W 10 S
Notice that there are two prepositions in 7, and both are strong forms.

6 Rewind and repeat. Pause at the end of each sentence to give students time to repeat. During repetition, monitor the pronunciation of the prepositions.

Try to elicit from students that strong forms are used:
a) when the prepositions end a sentence (examples 1, 4, 5, 8 and 10);
b) when they are intended to contrast with another preposition (example 7).

7 On the recording:
From my home in Birmingham, first I'm going to the north of England. I'm going to stay in Durham at the Cumbria Hotel. I'm going to stay there for three days. Then I'm going to drive from Durham to Cambridge. I'm going to stay at the Monarch Hotel for two days. Then I'm going to drive to the west of England. I'm going to stay at the Clifton Guest House in Bristol for three days. From Bristol I'm going to drive to Brighton and stay at the Promenade Hotel for two days. After that I'm going to drive home again.

8 The starting point for the planned journey could be anywhere in Britain. If students are already studying in Britain, then the starting point could be the place where they are studying. Or they could imagine they are arriving in Britain by air or sea.

You may find it useful to demonstrate this first with a better student. Point out that students should use similar language to that in the example ('I'm going to …', 'to drive from … to …', 'to drive to …', 'for … days', etc.). This will provide plenty of opportunity to produce prepositions. During pairwork, monitor the prepositions *at, for, from, of* and *to*.

Unit 56 The pronunciation of '-ed' endings

1 On the recording (Jane Bradbury – JB; Friend – FR):
JB: I saw a terrible accident last week.
FR: Why, what <u>happened</u>?
JB: Well, I was working in my office. I <u>wanted</u> to see what the weather was like so I <u>walked</u> over to the window and I <u>looked</u> outside.
FR: And what did you see?
JB: Well, nothing at first. But then a car came along the road. It <u>stopped</u> at the crossing opposite my office. A man and a woman <u>started</u> to cross when another car drove straight over the crossing without even slowing down.
FR: Oh, no! Was anybody hurt?
JB: Well, the woman <u>jumped</u> out of the way and the car just <u>missed</u> her. But it <u>knocked</u> down the man.
FR: So what did you do?
JB: Well, after that I <u>phoned</u> for an ambulance and the police and then I went outside.
FR: Did it take long for them to come?
JB: No, they <u>arrived</u> in just two or three minutes. The ambulance

men <u>helped</u> the woman to stand up. I think she was OK. But they <u>carried</u> the man into the ambulance on a stretcher. I <u>explained</u> what I'd seen to the police.

FR: And what about the driver?

JB: Well, apparently they <u>arrested</u> a man for dangerous driving.

The headline '**Man injured by car on crossing**' best summarises what happened.

2 Rewind and let the students hear the story again. This task could be done in a number of ways. One way is for students to close their books and attempt to retell the story without the prompts and words given. Perhaps ask one student to start and when this student has contributed some of the story, ask another to continue. Alternatively, ask students to retell the story making use of the prompts and words. Then, at a later stage – perhaps at the end of the lesson or on a following day – ask them to try to retell it from memory without the prompts and words. Another possibility is for students to work in pairs and for one to retell the story to their partner. Choose a method that is most appropriate for your class. Whatever method you choose, monitor the pronunciation of the past tense '-ed' endings.

3 Monitor the pronunciation of '-ed' endings.

4 *Answers*

/t/	/d/	/ɪd/
walked	explained	wanted
knocked	phoned	arrested
jumped	arrived	started
looked		carried
stopped		
helped		
missed		

Background

The rules for pronouncing '-ed' endings are as follows:
1 It is pronounced /ɪd/ after verbs that end with /t/ or /d/ or that have the letter 'y' changed to 'i' in their simple past tense forms.
2 It is pronounced /t/ after /p/, /tʃ/, /k/, /f/, /s/ and /ʃ/ (voiceless consonants).
3 It is pronounced /d/ after all other sounds.

5 Point out that 'carried' is an exception. In verbs that end with a consonant followed by the letter 'y', 'y' is changed to 'i' in the simple past tense form and '-ed' is pronounced /ɪd/.

6 Monitor the pronunciation of past tense '-ed' endings.

Unit 57 More on the pronunciation of '-ed' endings

1 *Answers*

1 rained	2 dropped	3 polluted	4 arrived / posted
5 finished	6 passed	7 laughed	8 mended 9 washed
10 walked			

Notice that all the verbs to be replaced are either followed by a vowel or end the sentence. This highlights the three pronunciations of '-ed', avoiding any changes in their pronunciation caused by contact with a following consonant. (For more information on this see Unit 39.)

2 During repetition and pairwork monitor the pronunciation of past tense '-ed' endings.

3 The additions to the table in task **4**, Unit 56 are indicated below:

/t/	/d/	/ɪd/
k p s gh (pronounced /f/) sh	n v	t d

> **Extension**
>
> Ask students to find more past tense '-ed' words and to decide how the ending is pronounced. They can add letters to the table where necessary.

4 To add a competitive element, count the number of words used in each story ending in 'ed'. Students should try to use the maximum number possible while keeping the story coherent. You could set a time limit, too.

Example story on recording:
One day Tom woke up and realised that he was late for work. He washed, shaved and brushed his teeth. He hurried downstairs and walked quickly to the bus stop. He waited for about five minutes before the bus arrived. But when he got to his office he discovered that it was closed. Tom had forgotten that it was Sunday!

Select students to report their stories back to the class. Monitor the pronunciation of past tense '-ed' endings during the story telling.

Unit 58 The pronunciation of '-s' endings

> **Background**
>
> The rules for pronouncing the '-s' and 'es' endings are as follows:
> 1 It is pronounced /ɪz/ after /s/, /z/, /ʃ/, /ʒ/, /tʃ / and /dʒ/.

2 It is pronounced /s/ after /p/, /t/, /k/, /f/ and /θ/ (other voiceless consonants).

3 It is pronounced /z/ after all other sounds.

2 *Answers* (and pronunciation of endings)

		Odd one out	
1 looks, sleeps, cuts, hopes	(ending = /s/)	runs (ending = /z/)	
2 finishes, chooses, switches, washes	(/ɪz/)	includes	(/z/)
3 phones, gives, cleans, buys	(/z/)	teaches	(/ɪz/)
4 plays, stays, rains, happens	(/z/)	gets	(/s/)
5 forgets, sits, speaks, stops	(/s/)	touches	(/ɪz/)
6 begins, drives, seems, sells	(/z/)	promises	(/ɪz/)

3 Rewind and repeat. Pause at the end of each word to give students time to repeat and write a letter or letters in the table. During repetition, monitor the pronunciation of the word endings.

The completed table should look like this:

/z/			/s/			/ɪz/		
n	d	v	k	p	t	sh	s	ch
y	m	ll						

4 During pairwork, monitor the pronunciation of the '-s' and '-es' endings.

5 Add 'g' under /z/ and 'dg' under /ɪz/.

6 *Possible answers*
Newsagent's – cigarettes, matches
Shoe shop – shoes, slippers
Clothes shop – jeans, socks, gloves
Sweet shop – sweets
Supermarket – biscuits, cornflakes
Baker's – cakes
Hardware shop – nails
Greengrocer's – potatoes

If you think the names of shops may be a problem for your students, write these on the board before starting the exercise and explain what they mean.

Ask students to report back following the pattern:
    'You'd go to a ... to buy ...'
Monitor the pronunciation of '-s' or '-es' in the words given in the box.

Part 8 Pronouncing written words

Aims and organisation

In Part 8 students learn about some of the connections between
pronunciation and **written letters**. The rules that connect pronunciation
and written letters in English are very complex. In Part 8 students are
introduced to some that are fairly easy to understand and remember.

Unit 59
Shows that the number of letters and sounds in a word may be
different. Shows that consonant letters usually represent only one
sound and gives practice in identifying consonants at the beginnings of
words.

Unit 60
Pronouncing the letters 'c' and 'g'.

Unit 61
Pronouncing the consonant pair 'th'.

Unit 62
Pronouncing the consonant pairs 'sh', 'ch' and 'gh'.

Unit 63
Spelling the vowel sound /ə/ (as in <u>a</u>cross).

Unit 64
Pronouncing the single vowel letters 'a', 'e', 'i', 'o' and 'u'.

Unit 65
Pronouncing vowel pairs such as 'oa' and 'ei'.

Unit 66
Letters that are not pronounced.

General notes

Three sources of information on sound-spelling relationships are
recommended. (See the list of *Recommended books* on page 3.)
Gimson (1989) lists possible spellings of each of the sounds of English
together with example words. Wells (1990) lists possible
pronunciations of each of the letters of English together with example
words. Kenworthy (1987, Ch. 5) gives a brief introduction to the

English spelling system, a concise set of rules for the pronunciation of English letters, and some suggestions for teaching.

Notes on each unit

Unit 59 Letters and sounds

1 *Answers*

	S	D		S	D		S	D
fog	☑	☐	winter	☐	☑	not	☑	☐
luck	☐	☑	shut	☐	☑	thin	☐	☑
cough	☐	☑	chess	☐	☑	other	☐	☑
cut	☑	☐	bill	☐	☑	touch	☐	☑
plan	☑	☐	dust	☑	☐			

Extension

For better students, or as an extension to this task, ask students to decide how many letters and how many sounds are in each word. Answers for this are:

	Number of letters	Number of sounds		Number of letters	Number of sounds
fog	3	3	chess	5	3
luck	4	3	bill	4	3
cough	5	3	dust	4	4
cut	3	3	not	3	3
plan	4	4	thin	4	3
winter	6	5	other	5	3
shut	4	3	touch	5	3

2 During repetition monitor the pronunciation of the words.

3 *Answers*

b ①   f ①   k ①   n ①   s ②   w ①
c ②   g ②   l ①   p ①   t ①
d ①   h ①   m ①   r ①   v ①

Three letters are commonly pronounced in one of two ways:
'c' can be pronounced /k/ (cat) or /s/ (police)
'g' can be pronounced /g/ (gram) or /dʒ/ (age)
's' can be pronounced /s/ (spin) or /z/ (visa)

4 This is a 'round-the-class' activity. Point out that the last letter of each word is the same as the first letter of the next and then ask for ways of continuing the chain given in the book. Start the next chain by giving a word yourself and asking for a suggestion for the next word. Continue to ask for suggestions as the chain grows or nominate students. Wrong words or repetitions mean elimination. Keep a note of words that cause problems and at the end check that students can pronounce them correctly.

Unit 60 Pronouncing consonant letters 'c' and 'g'

1 & 2 *Answers*

a) The traffi©'s bad in the çity çentre.

b) After the çinema, we went to a dis©o.

c) I've been to Ameri©a twiçe.

d) Only take this mediçine in an emergençy.

e) I went a©ross the road to the post offiçe.

f) I had to ©olle©t a parçel.

g) I haven't had a çigarette sinçe De©ember.

h) ©all the poliçe!

3 During repetition monitor the pronunciation of the letter 'c' in these sentences.

4 The letter 'c' is pronounced /s/ before the letters 'e', 'i' or 'y' in a word, and pronounced /k/ everywhere else.

5 The exceptions are:
together, girl, begin, give, get
During repetition monitor the pronunciation of the letter 'g'.

6 Students should monitor each other's pronunciation of the letter 'g'.

> **Extension**
> Ask students for other words that contain either the letter 'c' or the letter 'g'. List them on the board and tell students to group them either into words that follow the rules that they have learned in this unit, or the exceptions.

Unit 61 Pronouncing 'th'

> **Background**
> Relevant rules for the pronunciation of 'th' are as follows:
> 1 At the beginning of words 'th' is pronounced /θ/ as in think except in some common grammar words. These include: the, they, them, their, this, that, these, those, than, there, though.
> 2 At the ends of words 'th' is nearly always pronounced /θ/ (for example, bath, path, month, mouth, north, south, tooth).

3 When it comes in the middle of a word, a useful rule (though not always correct) to tell you how to pronounce 'th' in common words is that it is pronounced /ð/ in words where it comes before an '-er' ending (for example, brother, mother, father, either, together, weather, other) and /θ/ when it does not (for example, athletics, author, cathedral, mathematics, sympathy).

1 Point out that this rule applies only to the consonant pair 'th' at the *beginning* of words.

2 *Answers*

How many are there?	A thousand.
What's the matter?	I'm thirsty.
Is this yours?	Yes, thank you.
What time's their train?	At three twenty-five.
Where are they?	Through here.
Is he fatter than me?	No, he's thinner.
What day are you going there?	On Thursday.

3 After listening, rewind and repeat. Pause at the end of each sentence to give students time to repeat. During repetition monitor the pronunciation of 'th'.

4 When 'th' is at the end of a word it is pronounced /θ/.

5 'th' is pronounced /ð / in: father, other, weather, together, either and rather.
'th' in the middle of a word is usually pronounced /ð/ if the word ends in 'er'.

6 During repetition monitor the pronunciation of 'th'.

7 When students report their decisions monitor /θ/ and /ð/ pronunciations. /θ/ is particularly common in saying dates, e.g. the thirteenth of July nineteen thirty.

Answers
Josef Stalin died – 5th March 1953; State of Malaysia was created – 16th September 1963; Mrs Thatcher became Prime Minister – 3rd May 1979; John McEnroe won Wimbledon – 3rd July 1983; Pablo Picasso died – 8th April 1973; the first football World Cup began in Uruguay – 13th July 1930.

Extension

You can provide practice, particularly of /θ/, with almost any activity in which students are required to give dates. For example, ask students to give the full forms of dates such as 13/1/1933 (the thirteenth of January nineteen thirty-three). Or you could simply ask the students to give their own date of birth.
  More practice of /θ/ and /ð/ can be found in Part 2, Unit 13.

Unit 62 Pronouncing 'sh', 'ch' and 'gh'

Background

Relevant information on the pronunciation of 'ch', 'gh' and 'sh' is as follows:

1 'ch' is usually pronounced /tʃ/, and almost always pronounced this way after the letter 't' (e.g. match) and at the end of a word (e.g. rich). It can also be pronounced /ʃ/ (e.g. machine) and /k/ (e.g. chemistry).

2 'gh' can be pronounced /g/ (e.g. ghost), /f/ (e.g. rough), or silently after the letter 'i' (e.g. high) and some other vowels (e.g. through).

3 'sh' is always pronounced /ʃ/ (e.g. ship).

1 *Answers*

  1 one

  2 machine

  3 Possible answers: tough, rough, cough, laugh

  4 Possible answers: night, high

  5 ghost

2 During repetition monitor the pronunciation of 'sh', 'ch' and 'gh' in these words.

3 *Possible answers*

1 shampoo, toothbrush	6 shop, church
2 cheese, fish	7 ship, fish
3 shoes, shirt	8 tough, fresh
4 washing machine, dishwasher	9 Chinese, British
5 ʒhiver, cough	10 rough, sharp

4 During reporting back monitor pronunciation of the letter pairs 'sh', 'ch' and 'gh'.

5 To make this task a little easier, give some 'key words' to help students complete the sentences. There are various possibilities, but these might include:

  1 When ... tennis?   4 What ... shopping?

  2 How ... pay?   5 Why ... so hungry?

  3 Why ... phone?

During performance, monitor the pronunciation of 'ch', 'gh' and 'sh' in B's parts.

Unit 63 Pronunciation, spelling and word stress

Background

For more information on the pronunciation of vowels in unstressed syllables, see the notes for Part 4, Unit 32.

1 The underlined vowels are all pronounced /ə/.

2 & 3 *Answers*

daught(er)   camer(a)   comp(a)ny   c(o)ndition   petr(o)l

neighb(our)   hands(o)me   (a)broad   Engl(a)nd   doct(or)

pr(o)nunciation

During repetition monitor the pronunciation of /ə/ in these words.

4 Monitor the pronunciation of /ə/.

5 *Answers*

supp(er)   s<u>upp</u>ose   c(o)mmercial   <u>comm</u>(o)n   c(o)ll<u>ect</u>

c(o)ll(ar)   conc<u>ert</u>   c(o)nt<u>inue</u>   <u>pers</u>(o)n   p(er)<u>cent</u>

Notice that if the first syllable is unstressed, then the vowel is pronounced 'schwa'. If it is stressed, it has another pronunciation.

6 /ə/ is the common pronunciation of <u>unstressed</u> syllables. It is never the vowel sound in <u>stressed</u> syllables.

7 Answers (the /ə/ vowel in each word is underlined): <u>a</u>dvertisem<u>e</u>nt, accid<u>e</u>nt, aer<u>o</u>plane, ambul<u>a</u>nce, bus driv<u>er</u>, childr<u>e</u>n, cigarette, cinem<u>a</u>, doct<u>o</u>r, ladd<u>e</u>r, letterbox, mot<u>or</u>bike, newsagent's, newspap<u>er</u>, passeng<u>er</u>s, pavem<u>e</u>nt, p<u>e</u>destri<u>a</u>n, petr<u>o</u>l stati<u>o</u>n, phot<u>o</u>graph<u>er</u>, p<u>o</u>licem<u>a</u>n, stretch<u>er</u>, sup<u>er</u>market, window clean<u>er</u>, wom<u>a</u>n.

Ways of spelling the sound /ə/ include: *or, e, a, o* and *er*.

Unit 64 Pronouncing single vowel letters

2 U.S.A. = The United States of America
E.C. = The European Community
P.T.O. = Please Turn Over
I.O.U. = I Owe You
U.N. = The United Nations
U.K. = The United Kingdom
U.A.E. = The United Arab Emirates
W.H.O.= The World Health Organisation

4 *Answers*
c<u>a</u>ke   fact   g<u>a</u>me   l<u>i</u>fe   tap   cup   test   h<u>o</u>me
th<u>e</u>se   left   bit   t<u>u</u>ne   spell   bag   drop
pl<u>a</u>ne   m<u>i</u>ne   t<u>u</u>be   soft   n<u>o</u>se   kill   dust

5 Monitor the pronunciation of the vowels.

6 Ask students to complete this table. Explain that V = a vowel letter (either 'a', 'e', 'i', 'o' or 'u'), C = a consonant letter and 'e' = the letter 'e'. For example, 'home' is C+V+C+e and 'soft' is C+V+C+C. When a one-syllable word ends with C+e (i.e. a single consonant followed by the letter 'e') the vowel letter is pronounced with its name.

Extension

As an additional exercise, ask students if the rule also applies to one-syllable words in which these vowels are followed by *two* consonant letters + the letter 'e'. Either ask them to provide examples or give them some, e.g. bridge, dance, else, France, fridge, horse, large, nurse, once, sense, since. The rule *doesn't* normally apply in such cases (and the rules for the pronunciation of vowels in these cases are complex), but there are a few exceptions which do follow the rule given, e.g. change, taste, waste.

Unit 65 Pronouncing vowel pairs

1 & 2 *Most likely answers*

1 three	5 between	9 eighteen	13 school
2 spoon	6 cheap	10 sleep	14 eat
3 wool	7 afternoon	11 easy	15 already
4 clean	8 cooking	12 heavy	16 break

3 *Answers* (students select one example word in each box from the ones shown here)

	/iː/	/uː/	/e/	/ʊ/	/eɪ/
'ee'	three, between, eighteen, sleep (4)	✘	✘	✘	✘
'oo'	✘	spoon, afternoon, school (3)	✘	wool, cooking (2)	✘
'ea'	clean, cheap, easy, eat (4)	✘	heavy, already (2)	✘	break (1)

Pronouncing the vowel pair 'ou'

4 Play the conversation twice. The first time, play it through without stopping. Then replay it, pausing at the ends of sentences to give students time to write in the words from the box.

Answers

A: How was the holiday?
B: Marvellous.
A: Switzerland, wasn't it?
B: That's right. It's a beautiful country.
A: Did a group of you go?
B: No, just me and my cousin.
A: Where did you stay?
B: We rented a house in Zurich.

A: How was the weather?

B: Well, a bit <u>cloudy</u>.

A: Lots of shopping?

B: Oh, yes. Lots of <u>souvenirs</u>. And I <u>found</u> this <u>blouse</u>.

A: Lovely. Did you go skiing, too?

B: Yes, we went <u>south</u> to the <u>mountains</u>.

A: I've never been skiing. It <u>sounds</u> too <u>dangerous</u>.

B: Well, I had a few falls, but nothing too <u>serious</u>.

A: And will you go back?

B: Probably. The only <u>trouble</u> was, there were too many <u>tourists</u>!
But you've been on holiday, too, haven't you? How was <u>yours</u>?

A: Oh, we had a really good time…

5 During repetition and pairwork, monitor the pronunciation of the words in the box.

6 The words in the conversation containing the vowel pair 'ou' are as follows:

1 marvellous, dangerous, serious   /ə/
2 country, cousin, trouble   /ʌ/
3 group, you, souvenirs   /uː/
4 house, cloudy, found, blouse, south, mountains, sounds   /aʊ/
5 tourists, yours   /ɔː/

They are grouped here according to their pronunciation.

Note that the 'ou' in *tourists* and *yours* is pronounced /ɔː/ by some speakers and /ʊə/ by others.

7 During pairwork, monitor the pronunciation of vowel pairs. The vowel pairs in the questions given are underlined below.

Do you prefer …

a) to stay in your own <u>country</u> or go <u>abroad</u>?

b) to travel by <u>boat</u> or by <u>coach</u>?

c) to <u>sleep</u> a lot or get up <u>early</u> and <u>see</u> lots of places?

Do you prefer staying in a place …

d) <u>near</u> <u>mountains</u> or <u>near</u> the <u>coast</u>?

e) with dry but <u>cool</u> <u>weather</u> or wet but hot <u>weather</u>?

f) with a swimming <u>pool</u> or a <u>beach</u>?

Unit 66 Silent letters

1 *Answers*

cup(b)oard   clim(b)   (k)nee   is(l)and   hal(f)   autum(n)

(k)now   han(d)kerchief   lis(t)en   (k)nife   (h)our   t(w)o

Chris(t)mas   ans(w)er   com(b)   (h)onest   ta(l)k   han(d)some

For the second part of the task, rewind the tape and repeat. Pause at the end of each word to give students time to repeat. During repetition, monitor pronunciation. Check that the circled letters are not pronounced.

2 Monitor pronunciation. Check that the words listed are said in their 'normal speed' form.

3 *Answers*

int(e)resting   p(o)lice   choc(o)late   secret(a)ry   fact(o)ry

sev(e)ral   av(e)rage   pos(t)man   diff(e)rent   fam(i)ly

gover(n)ment   med(i)cine   strawb(e)rries   asp(i)rin

dus(t)bin   fav(ou)rite

4 Monitor the pronunciation of the words above. Check that the words are said in their normal form with sounds deleted.

5 *Answers*

How often do you play football?	Twice a week on average.
Would you like some sweets?	I've already had some chocolate.
What's on the news?	The government's resigned.
We've been robbed!	Call the police.
Who did you go on holiday with?	I went with my family.
What shall we have for pudding?	Strawberries and ice cream.
What's in the bottle?	Some medicine for my cold.
What do you think of this cheese?	It's my favourite.
Are these packets the same?	No, they're different.
Have you ever been to Paris?	Several times.

While the pairs are saying the conversations, monitor the pronunciation of the words listed in 3 above.

6 Students have to write two-line conversations. The words on the left should be in the first part and the words on the right in the second. While students say the conversations they have written, monitor the pronunciation of the words on the right.

Some possible conversations might be:
2 A: Have we had any letters?
   B: The postman's just come.
3 A: Where do you work?
   B: In a car factory.
4 A: What can I take for my headache?
   B: There are some aspirins in the cupboard.
5 A: What shall I do with this rubbish?
   B: Put it in the dustbin.
6 A: Who typed this letter?
   B: The new secretary.